KILLING SELENA AND OTHER STORIES

ANGIE DAVISON

Killing Selena

Angie Davison

Published by Trellis Publishing, 2021.

KILLING SELENA

First edition. July 3, 2021.

Copyright © 2021 Angie Davison.

ISBN: 979-8224509195

Written by Angie Davison.

Yolanda Saldivar

"I took it out to tell her 'Look I'm going to kill myself' and she said 'No Yolanda' and she turned to open the door to – to call for help or something...and I told her 'No' and I just – and I – I never pointed a gun at anybody and it just went off...I bought this gun to kill myself. Not her. Not her. And she told me 'Yolanda, I don't want you to kill yourself.' And we were talking about it when I took it out and pointed it to my head. And when I pointed it to my head, she opened the door. I said 'Selena close that door,' and when I said that the gun went off."[1]

In order to learn more about Yolanda Saldivar, it is necessary to know about the woman she murdered – Selena Quintanilla, because the murder was, by itself, unremarkable. However, the victim was a beloved singer who was idolized by many, and her untimely death propelled Saldivar firmly into the spotlight. Their lives were intertwined, and as such one cannot tell the story of one without telling the story of the other.

Selena Quintanilla – Her Background

Selena Quintanilla was born in Lake Jackson, Texas, on April 16th, 1971.[2] Her mother, Marcella Samora, was born in 1944, of half Mexican-American and half Cherokee-Indian descent. Her father, Abraham Jr was born in 1939, in Corpus Christi, Texas.

The couple met in 1961 when Abraham Jr was in the military, and they married in 1963.

In 1963 Marcella gave birth to the couple's first child, Abraham III, who was followed four years later in 1967 by Suzette. Selena's birth, in 1971 completed the Quintanilla family.

1963 was a busy year for the Quintanillas – not only did they get married and have their first child, but Abraham Jr was also discharged from the military, and they settled down to married life.[3]

After leaving the military, Abraham Jr took a steady job at Dow Chemical as a shipping clerk, a job which gave the family a fairly comfortable life.

However, Abraham's passion had always been music. When he was younger he had been a singer in a band called Los Dinos (the boys) and when he heard Selena sing for the first time at the age of around six he knew that music was still running through the family's veins.

Abraham loved all kinds of music and encouraged all three of his children to be the same. The Quintanilla children would get together in their spare time and practice their music as often as they could, albeit reluctantly at times because music practice meant less time for playing.

The Quintanillas were ambitious, and in 1980 Abraham Jr left his safe and steady job at Dow Chemical to open a family restaurant.

PapaGayos opened in the early 1980s, with Abraham pouring all of the family's savings into it. It seemed like a good investment – not only did it serve Mexican food and was the only one of its type in the area, but it also provided a venue for Selena to showcase her talents.[4]

By the time the restaurant opened, Abraham had formed a family band, which he called "Selena y Los Dinos", a play on the name of his former band. They would play at weekends in the restaurant, and would also perform at weddings and other parties.

Tejano music, which was the style the band played, was a mix of genres – rock and roll combined with Mexican. Abraham Jr began writing music for the band, original songs which, in keeping with the theme, were in Spanish. English was Selena's first language, so she had to learn the lyrics phonetically, a painstaking task.

While Selena sang in the band, Suzette played the drums and Abraham III was on bass guitar. However, the recession of 1983 hit them hard, and the restaurant was forced to close.

The Quintanillas lost everything, including their home.

Their one glimmer of hope was the children's talent, and in particular, Selena. Abraham Jr appointed himself as the band's manager, and he put the children to work at weddings, fairs, birthday parties and even busking on street corners. Although the band was gaining popularity, financially the family was still suffering – they had to depend on handouts and food stamps, and were living with eight other relatives. Circumstances were far from ideal – the home they all shared had only one bathroom and space was limited.

It was a gruelling regimen – Selena was studying at school by day, and performing by night, but her determination paid off and she earned her diploma.

The band used a tour bus to travel around, and in the early days, they would have to perform along the way to pay for their gas and food. But things started to pick up when, in 1984, they recorded and released their first album *Selena y Los Dinos*.

Things took off rapidly following that first success – in the next four years, the family had produced a further five albums, which, in the male-dominated field of Tejano music, made her something of a trailblazer for girls everywhere. So much so, in fact, that she won the Female Vocalist of the Year for ten years running from the Tejano Music Awards.

Things went from strength to strength for Selena – during the last part of the 80s to the beginnings of the 90s, Selena was lauded as the new Gloria Estefan. She released her first studio album, *Selena*, in 1989, landed a $75,000 contract with Coca-Cola as their spokesperson in Texas, her brother, Abraham, became her record producer, and perhaps most importantly of all, she met Chris Perez.

Chris was the band's new guitarist, and the pony-tailed musician would also go on to become Selena's husband.[5]

The relationship was not without its problems. Selena's father didn't like Perez's image and felt it might jeapordize the band's popularity, but Abraham III persuaded his father to keep Perez on. When Selena landed her contract with Coca-Cola, Abraham Jr treated the entire band to a vacation in Acapulco, and it was during this time that Perez's feelings for Selena began to grow. However, he already had a girlfriend and tried to keep his distance from Selena. The attraction was mutual though, and the pair became an item, hiding the relationship from Selena's father.

It was Suzette, Selena's sister, who blew the whistle on the couple, and Abraham Jr was furious, banning Perez from seeing his daughter anymore. In public, this became the case, but in private the relationship continued.

Abraham Jr was an astute man, however, and it didn't take him long to put two and two together. During a journey on the band's tour bus, he stormed to the back where the couple was sitting and an argument broke out between Selena and her father. Perez tried to calm things down, but this inflamed the situation more and Abraham Jr threatened to break up the band if the relationship continued. This had the desired effect, and Perez was fired from the band.

Selena was suffering without Perez though. She felt that the only way Perez would ever be accepted into the family and the band would be if the pair got married, and on April 2nd, 1992 Selena hammered on Perez's door and told him they should get married that day, that it was the only way. Perez wanted to do things 'the right way' but Selena insisted that her father would never accept it, so the pair eloped and got married in Nueces County, Texas.

The plan was to keep things quiet for a while, but, as is often the way, the media found out and announced the marriage a few short hours after the ceremony. Abraham Jr was appalled, and for a while, he distanced himself from his daughter.

It wasn't until Selena and Chris moved into their own apartment that Abraham Jr backed down and asked Perez to re-join the band.[6]

Yolanda Saldivar

Frank and Juanita Saldivar had seven children, the youngest of whom was Yolanda who was born on September 19th, 1960 in San Antonio, Texas. The Saldivars were normal, working class people – Frank worked hard as a head waiter at Jacala – a West End Mexican restaurant.[7]

Saldivar has an unremarkable background. Periodically bullied because of her weight, she was something of a loner – she had very few friends and never took part in any kind of social activities. Such was her 'unremarkability' that few fellow students can even recall Saldivar at school.

Having attended several schools, Saldivar went on to the University of Texas, followed by Palo Alto College where she studied to become a Registered Nurse, fulfilling her dream in December 1990 when she was given a Bachelor of Science in Nursing from Texas A&M International University.

Saldivar worked hard as a nurse at Medical Center Hospital, earning $60,000 per year. She had never married but was the adoptive mother of three children, and after their adoption, she had to work part-time in order to look after them.

Money was always a thorn in Yolanda Saldivar's side – Dr Faustino Gomez, a dermatologist and former employer of Saldivar sued her for $9,200 which he claimed she had stolen from him while working for him. Luckily for Saldivar, the case was settled out of court, but just two months later she was back in court, this time over her failure to repay $7,361, a student loan obtained through the Texas Guaranteed Student Loan Corporation. By then, Saldivar was working as a nurse at St. Luke's Lutheran Hospital.

In the following four years, Saldivar began losing her faith in the nursing profession. She had worked at two further hospitals in that time, but her interest was waning.

But while her interest in her profession was on a downward slide, her interest in Tejano music was growing. After attending a concert by another Tejano singer, Shelley Lares, she approached the singer and asked her about the possibility of opening up and running an official fan club. Lares' father would only entertain the idea of family working with the singer, however, and refused his permission.

So Saldivar turned her attention to Selena Quintanilla. In the beginning, Saldivar had a strong dislike for Selena. She didn't like the dominance Selena had over the Tejano music scene, or how she continually won the awards associated with the genre. But she was persuaded to go along to one of Selena's concerts and her opinions changed.

Saldivar then approached Abraham Jr, Selena's father, with the same proposal she had made to Shelley Lares – that she set up and run an official fan club. This time her proposition was accepted, and the Selena fan club was born, with Yolanda Saldivar at its helm as the official club President.[8]

A Professional Association

In sharp contrast to Selena's beauty, Saldivar was short, heavy set, and 11 years Selena's senior, but her enthusiasm endeared her to the Quintanilla family.

Selena grew very fond of her new associate, and the pair quickly became friends. She could see immediately what a good job Saldivar was doing with the fan club.

"She's doing exceptionally well...fan clubs can ruin you if people get upset and turned off by them. But she's doing really good."

In return for Saldivar's good work and diligence, Selena bought the older woman gifts. Suddenly the former 'nobody' had been thrust into a life she had only dreamed of, and she loved the attention.

One of Saldivar's passions was all things cow-related, so Selena bought her a rug which was covered in cow print, at a cost of $800, along with a 'cow phone' in Los Angeles. Saldivar lapped up the attention.

A little too much, according to many observers.

Saldivar kept a life-sized cardboard figure of the singer in her home, which she covered with backstage passes.[9]

Her home slowly turned into a shrine to Selena, with candles burning around photos of the singer, and posters on the walls. In 1995 reporters from *The Dallas Morning News* actually stated that the fan club President was bordering on obsession.[10]

As time went on, Selena decided to diversify and launched *Selena Etc.*, a chain of stores which not only sold Selena's own line of clothing and jewelry but also had a hair and beauty salon within. It was a lot of work, and Selena turned to the one person she trusted to take over the helm of her business venture – Yolanda Saldivar.

Saldivar was delighted. The fan club had been a voluntary, unpaid position, but this new job was a salaried one, not to mention the kudos associated with it.[11]

Things Turn Sour

Yolanda was not a skilled communicator when it came to dealing with people. Her childhood and youth had been spent mostly in a self-imposed isolation, so when she found herself suddenly thrust into the business world, she began to flounder. In particular, Saldivar appeared to have a grave dislike for Selena's designer, Martin Gomez.

Gomez and Saldivar shared an office together for eight months before the designer quit his job as he found working with Saldivar to be completely untenable.

"She was very vindictive. She was very possessive of Selena...She'd get, like, very angry if you crossed her. She would play so many mind games, say people had said things they hadn't said. So many things would happen to the clothing I was working on. I knew that I had finished a certain piece, but I would come back from a trip to New York and the hems would be ripped out. It was very strange."

Saldivar ingratiated herself with Selena more and more. She had a key to the home the star shared with her husband, Chris Perez, and access to the financial accounts of the business.

Gomez had his suspicions over Saldivar's use, or misuse, of Selena's money. She had a penchant for rental cars, and prior to a trip to Mexico, she had bought herself a lot of new clothes.

She had also, according to Gomez, tried to frame others for missing funds, including the designer himself. Some models hadn't received payment for their work, and Saldivar told Abraham Jr that the cheque he had given to her to pay the models' wages had been passed on to Gomez and that it was he who had 'lost' the money – an accusation he denies.

Selena treated all of her staff equally well, but as Saldivar's obsession grew she began to take Selena's attention as favoritism. It got to the point where nobody could speak to or approach Selena without going through Saldivar first.

She obviously had a problem with Gomez. On one occasion she confronted him, asking him if he thought he was better that she was, and whether, if she had money, would he like her. Gomez found her deeply unpleasant.

She liked to take the credit for others' hard work, too. On one occasion she made Gomez's assistant clean and tidy Selena's filing cabinets, but when she could see how delighted Selena was, she claimed responsibility for the work herself.

After Gomez left he warned Selena to be careful around Saldivar, describing her as evil. So much so, in fact, that he admitted he was, himself, afraid of her.[12]

It wasn't just Gomez who left the company under Saldivar's 'rule'. By December 1994, the staff had shrunk from 38 to 14, mostly because it was almost impossible to work with the woman. She would fire anyone she didn't like, which was most of the staff, and as soon as anyone dared to cross her, they were gone. The staff who did remain took their concerns to Selena, but she refused to believe that Saldivar, whom she had considered a friend, would or could behave like that. Not getting any relief from Selena, the employees then approached Abraham Jr, and told him of their concerns and misgivings. Abraham was more amenable to their grievances and spoke to his daughter, warning her that her 'friend' might be dangerous. Selena, once again, was deaf to the warnings about Saldivar and would not entertain the fact that there was anything amiss about her behavior. In fact, she blamed the situation on her father's inherent lack of trust in people.

Even Selena's own cousin, Debra Ramirez, quit the business after only a week.

The dissatisfaction was not only among the staff working directly in the boutiques. On a visit to the clothing factory where the Selena Etc clothes were made, the seamstress there was told by Saldivar that she could either agree with her or leave. She made enemies wherever she went.

Found Out

Things began to take a rapid downward spiral for Yolanda Saldivar in January 1995, when angry fans began to call and write to Abraham Jr, demanding to know why, despite having paid their membership fees, they had received nothing. Their enrolment fees promised them some items of Selena memorabilia, but it had failed to materialize.

Abraham Jr began to look into the fan club and the business and discovered that Saldivar had skimmed more than $30,000 from the fan club and boutiques.

Selena had to listen now.

Abraham called a meeting between himself, Selena, her sister Suzette, and Saldivar and presented the evidence he had gathered. According to Abraham, Saldivar merely stared at him as he accused her, without answering a single question. In fact, he got no reaction at all until he told Saldivar that unless she could come up with an explanation for the missing money he would call the police. As Saldivar wordlessly stormed out of the room, Suzette called after her, labelling her a liar and a thief.

Selena could no longer ignore what friends and family had been telling her. Following a heated argument on the phone the following day between Selena and Saldivar, the singer finally conceded to her husband, Chris Perez, that she could no longer trust Saldivar. However, she couldn't terminate the friendship because Saldivar was crucial in the expansion of the clothing line into Mexico, and she was also in possession of some important business papers.

Just a few days later, on March 13th, 1995 Yolanda Saldivar walked into *A Place to Shoot*, a gun store and firing range located in South San Antonio. She told the clerk that she needed protection from a relative of a patient she was caring for in her job as a nurse for terminally ill patients. When she left, she had a .38 caliber revolver and .38 caliber hollow point bullets in her purse. Hollow point bullets are designed to maximize the damage caused by a gunshot to the victim.

Yolanda Saldivar meant business.[13]

In the interim, following Saldivar's dismissal, she tried to assert her innocence to Selena, claiming she did indeed have the documents and receipts which would prove her innocence.

However, she remained unable to produce these documents. Then, towards the end of March 1995, Saldivar told Selena that she had been kidnapped, beaten, and raped and that her car had been stolen. The papers which would prove her innocence just so happened to have been in the car and were now missing.

Selena was concerned for her former friend and insisted on taking her to the hospital for an examination and treatment. Before the examination could even begin, Saldivar admitted that she had lied and that there had been no kidnapping, no beating and no rape. And there were no missing papers.

Selena finally realized that it was not going to be possible to retain any modicum of friendship with Saldivar, and the older woman knew it.[14]

Time Runs Out

On Thursday, March 30th, 1995 Saldivar made a call to Selena, telling her she was staying at the Days Inn Motel. She wanted to talk about what had happened and asked Selena if she would meet her in room 158. Selena agreed but went against Saldivar's wishes that she go alone.

Chris Perez accompanied his wife to the motel and stayed outside in the car while Selena went in. After some time Selena returned to the car but discovered that there were still some papers missing from the pile that Saldivar had supplied her with. The couple decided not to confront Saldivar again that day, and they went home.

The following day Selena returned to the Days Inn, but this time she was alone. She knocked on the door of room 158 and entered.[15]

Just before noon the same day – March 31st, 1995, Selena ran out of the motel room, screaming. A maid who was working at the hotel said that when she heard the calls for help she looked up and saw Saldivar shoot Selena in the back. Despite her wound, Selena managed to run to the lobby, before collapsing.

Emergency services received a call at around 11.50 am reporting that a gun had been fired and paramedics were immediately dispatched to the motel. Before Selena lost consciousness she was able to tell those around her that it had been Yolanda Saldivar who had pulled the trigger.

Selena was rushed to Memorial Medical Center, but despite having a transfusion of five pints of blood, (which was against her father's religious beliefs) Selena could not be saved, and she died at 1.05 pm.

The Aftermath

After Selena had fled room 158, Saldivar had also run, but police found her still in the parking lot in her pickup truck. For the next ten hours, Saldivar held a gun to her own head, threatening suicide and keeping the police at arm's length. Eventually, she was talked down, and arrested for the murder of Selena Quintanilla-Perez.

On October 23rd, 1995, Yolanda Saldivar was found guilty of murder and sentenced to life imprisonment with no possibility of parole for at least 30 years. It only took the jury two hours to reach their verdict.

Life inside is a lonely affair for the woman who once enjoyed the trappings of wealth and popularity on the back of Selena's success. The singer was hugely popular and well-loved, and Saldivar has been the target of many death threats while inside the prison, from fellow inmates who were fans of Selena. She spends 23 hours a day alone in her prison cell at the Mountain View Unit in Gatesville, with a two-hour visit from family allowed each week.

Her only company is a radio, which she was given permission to buy while inside the prison.

Saldivar has never admitted guilt for the murder. She has always claimed that she had been intending to kill herself instead, but that the gun had gone off accidentally, hitting Selena in the upper back and rupturing an artery. This explanation was disproved during the trial, though, when it was found that in order for the gun to be fired 11 pounds of pressure needed to be applied to the trigger.

As the years since her imprisonment have gone on, Saldivar's story has changed and evolved. She claimed that she had been protecting Selena and that she had items proving Selena had been cheating on her husband, Chris Perez - among them a diary, a letter, and some videos. The alleged lover, Ricardo Martinez, who worked for Selena, vehemently denied the accusations. But, according to Saldivar, Selena had entrusted her with a suitcase full of clothes which were to be kept by Saldivar until the opportunity arose for Selena to run away with her lover.[16]

Nobody but Yolanda Saldivar knows what happened inside room 158 that day, but whatever it was it resulted in the death of a beloved icon and turned Yolanda Saldivar into one of the most hated women in the country. She will be eligible for parole in 2025, but even now, more than 20 years after the murder, feelings are still running high over Selena's murder. Perhaps the safest thing for Yolanda Saldivar would be to stay behind bars for the rest of her life, where Selena's many fans can't reach her.

KILLER SISTERS : THE TRUE STORY OF THE ROBINSONS

AMY DELANEY

Holly and Ashleigh Robinson

When Antoni Robinson built his house in the 1970s for his wife, Susan Phillips, and their two daughters, Amanda and Claire, he was building more than a house – he was building a home. Somewhere to build memories.

Sadly, the marriage didn't last, and somewhere around 1980 the couple separated, and following his divorce, Antoni's Polish parents bought the bungalow from him and lived there for the next ten years.

Joanne Barr

Three or four years after his marriage ended, Antoni Robinson met Joanne Barr, and, when his mother died in 1992, Antoni bought the bungalow back, and once again it became home to his family – this time consisting of Joanne, and their two daughters, Holly and Ashleigh. But Antoni was a good father, and although Amanda and Claire had moved to the South of England, they had a close relationship and were in regular contact.[1]

The couple never married.

Antoni's daughters from his first marriage had misgivings about Joanne Barr – she was, after all, only three years older than his own daughter, Amanda. But they loved their dad and wanted to see him happy, so they put their misgivings aside and supported their father in his new relationship.

Things were going well – that is until Joanne had her own children with Antoni.

"At first, Joanne was lovely. But when she had her own kids, Ashleigh and Hollie, she changed towards us...she was jealous of Dad's first family. She was a possessive control freak and wouldn't let us near him...although I never liked her, she and Dad never knew that, I buried my feelings because Dad would have been devastated. Family was the most important thing to him."

Antoni revelled in his role as a father for the second time.

"He was overjoyed when Ashleigh and Hollie were born. He would do anything for them – always cleaning their shoes and making their dinner. He loved looking after them...he was so proud of them, particularly Ashleigh. She was so clever, gaining nine A-grade GCSEs. She was the apple of Dad's eye. If he was disappointed when she got pregnant at 18 instead of going to university, he never let on."[2]

Unhappy Marriage

Although the couple stayed together for 25 years, the relationship wasn't a happy one, and towards the end of 2009, Joanne Barr left the 3 bedroomed bungalow, taking the couple's two daughters with her.

That was not the end of the arguments which had blighted the relationship, however. If anything, Joanne, Ashleigh, and Holly moving out of the home in Colwyn Bay seemed to make things worse, and the rows escalated. So much so that Antoni went to stay with Amanda for a break.

"There were so many horrible arguments that Dad had a nervous breakdown and stayed with me for two weeks. Claire and I tried to get him back on his feet again."

But if Antoni thought that the break would do him good, he was mistaken.[3]

Plotting

While Amanda was trying to get her dad back on his feet, she received a phone call from her Aunt.

"Dad's sister phoned to say there was washing out on his line. Ashleigh had moved in while he was away."

But it wasn't the turning point Antoni would have liked. While their father was staying with Amanda, his youngest two daughters were busily making the bungalow their own. So when Antoni went home, it seriously cramped their style. Older daughter Amanda was horrified by their attitudes.

"The girls treated the house like their own pad and didn't want him back. They talked to him like an idiot and made him feel like a lodger in his own home.

"I hated hearing how they treated him, how they spoke to him. But I thought they were just being normal teenagers and hoped they'd grow out of it. I didn't imagine they had that kind of hatred for him."

Antoni returned to a house full – Ashleigh had moved in with her boyfriend, Gordon Harding, and their daughter who was seven months old at the time. Shortly after, Hollie also moved back in.[4]

The girls were on a mission. The bungalow had been put into joint names – both Antoni's and Joanne Barr's[5], and while Antoni was away, the girls went through his documents, including bank statements, and photocopied them all in order to give their mother as much ammunition as possible with which to fight him.

"Everything was relayed back to their mother. They were determined to get into his safe, which had bits of jewellery of sentimental value, and £900 cash."

The girls were demanding, but even when their father did give them what they wanted, it wasn't enough.

"[Ashleigh] had demanded £500 for intensive driving lessons, but Dad said he'd pay for weekly lessons instead...she was furious. He phoned me that night to say Ashleigh had been hateful towards him. It was a shock – Dad had never used a word like that about the girls before. What hurt him was that he'd spent the whole day working hard in the garden, but Ashleigh had made herself a sandwich and not offered him one. Something like that would have really hurt such a kind, selfless man like my dad."[6]

The next day, 61-year-old Antoni Robinson was dead.

Texts

Just a few days previously, an antiques dealer in Colwyn Bay was approached by two women in his shop, who asked whether or not Antoni Robinson had been in to sell any jewelry. More chillingly, Eagle

Star Insurance received a phone call from Joanne Barr, checking to see if Antoni had attempted to cash in the endowment policy on their house. The company confirmed to Barr that the policy was still in place.

Just hours later, on July 6th, 2010, a series of texts were exchanged between the two younger sisters – Ashleigh and Holly Robinson. Texts which showed the unfolding of a murder plot and began with three words from Holly:

"its game on."

What followed was their downfall (and written as the girls wrote them).

6.45 pm (Holly) "We getting the big guns out."

10 pm (Holly) "I knew you would do that."

10 pm: Ashleigh to Holly: "Wat?"

10.01 pm: (Holly) "Not let m cum."

10.01 pm: (Ashleigh) "Its just dangerous Holly."

10.02 pm: (Holly) "I can look out for myself."

10.03 pm: (Ashleigh) "Yeh fine i wil let u in then."

10.04 pm: (Holly) "Cool, you not guna help at all."

10.03 pm: (Ashleigh) "Prob nt."

10.13 pm: (Holly) "Why. You want it as much as me."

10.13 pm: (Ashleigh) "Yeh well i hve a baby to think."

10.14 pm: (Holly) "Well I wont do it ever, do what you want."

11.21 pm: (Ashleigh) "U must cum and go thru the bk."

11.22 pm: (Holly) "Is he bak?"

11.23 pm: (Ashleigh) "Nt yet i will txt u wen."

11.46 pm: (Ashleigh) "Hes hme xx."

11.47 pm: (Holly) "We will be on our way up soon x."

Midnight: (Ashleigh) "Where r u? N mum wi u?"

12.01 am: (Holly) "We are at home. Yeah why? x."

12.01 am: (Ashleigh) "Make sure sach has his fone. And show this 2 mum ok. Dad jus said tht he got rid of mum at crimbo an he;ll do the same to me cos it aint working out. Btw he is drinking coffee."

12.14 am: (Holly) "We're on our way. Hang tight. X"

12.17 am: (Ashleigh) "It's G. Head stright here and come."

12.21 am: (Ashleigh) "Keep ur mouth shut. Fone on silent."

12.22 am: (Ashleigh) "Dnt close gate either xx"

12.25 am: (Holly) "Ring me xx."

12.26 am: (Ashleigh) "We cnt. wats up?"

12.27 am: (Holly) "We're on our way. We are guna jump over the front gate, no houses, no witnesses."

12.32 am: (Holly) "Gate x."

12.34 am: (Ashleigh) "Wait at bottom of hill 4 ou."

12.35 am: (Ashleigh) "Wait 5 mins. G will txt u nxt xxx."

12.36 am: (Holly) "We are by the kitchen window."

12.37 am: (Ashleigh) "He has his light on i think."

12.38 am: (Ashleigh) "Light is off."[7]

The 'we' Holly Robinson was referring to was herself, and her boyfriend, 19-year-old Sacha Roberts. During the course of that text conversation, Sacha received two texts from Ashleigh's boyfriend, Gordon Harding, who was already at the house with her.

12.05am: Gordon Harding to Sacha: "Sash. He goes tonight. Need your backup."

and

12.38am: Gordon to Sacha: "Don't move 2 mins."

Less than half an hour after the last text was sent, Antoni Robinson was dead, and shortly afterwards one final text was sent – this time from Ashleigh to her mother, Joanne Barr:

"Things happened, he is no more. Sorry mum. xxxx."[8]

999 Call

Joanne Barr, having received the text from her daughter, Ashleigh, went to the former matrimonial home and took charge.[9] She called 999 and calmly told the operator that Antoni had been stabbed, and that although she hadn't checked, she presumed he was dead. She went on to tell the operator that Gordon Harding had stabbed Antoni because he had used threatening behaviour towards his girlfriend, Ashleigh, and their baby daughter.

When PC Rhian Evans arrived at the house, she found Ashleigh Robinson, Gordon Harding, Holly Robinson, and Sacha Roberts in the living room, huddled together and hugging one another.

As Joanne Barr had told the operator that Gordon Harding had stabbed Antoni Robinson, the police officer arrested him when she arrived, on suspicion of wounding. However, after she had seen the body and it became apparent that Antoni was dead, she re-arrested him on suspicion of murder.

When paramedics arrived, they found Antoni lying on his back on the bed, with his feet on the floor. He was not breathing and had no pulse, and an ECG test further confirmed that Antoni was deceased.[10]

Stabbed

Antoni Robinson had been stabbed 15 times in his face, neck, back and upper body. The injuries to his neck were so severe that the jugular vein on both sides of his neck had been severed, which would have led to him bleeding out and dying within a very short space of time. Forensics showed that at least two different knives had been used in the murder – a kitchen knife with a 3-inch blade and a bigger 7-inch blade on a commando-style weapon.[12]

Gordon Harding

Gordon Harding said that Antoni Robinson's death had been an accident – the result of self-defence. He admitted that he had gone into Robinson's bedroom to search for money and jewelry in Antoni's safe, but claimed that the 61-year-old man had woken up. He had taken the commando-style knife, he said, as a deterrent and to give him confidence. However, he claimed that when Antoni woke up, he had attacked Harding with a kitchen knife.

"He just came at me with it. I immediately grabbed his left wrist and we were struggling over the knife...I pulled my right hand up to my left

shoulder. That was the only place I could move to get away from him…he pulled my left wrist towards him and I cut him to the neck and to the rear of his right-hand shoulder."

The 20-year-old said that the night before the killing, Antoni had come home from the pub and an argument had ensued, which culminated in Antoni threatening to evict his daughter the next day. Harding's plan, according to him, was to search the safe and see if he could retrieve any documents which would enable Joanne Barr to move back into Antoni's bungalow.

"The door was closed. I opened it slightly… I opened it slowly trying not to make a noise. I started to move into the room."

He said that this was when Antoni woke up and 'lunged' at him.[13]

Following the murder, Harding removed his clothes, laid the two knives on top of the pile of blood-stained garments, and had a shower.

Sacha Roberts

19-year-old Sacha Roberts' role in the murder of Antoni Robinson is unclear. He was there, certainly, and admitted that he went along to support Gordon Harding, but he claims he never entered Antoni Robinson's bedroom. While standing on the landing outside the bedroom, Roberts said the door was open and he looked inside. As he stood watching, he said he saw Antoni Robinson lying in bed, and that Harding was standing over him. Before Harding had gone into the bedroom he had taken the combat knife from Roberts – the knife which Roberts had brought to the bungalow that night. He let Harding take the knife, thinking he would use it only to intimidate Robinson. But as he looked through the door at his friend standing over the older man, he saw his arm coming down again and again, and he realized that Robert Harding was stabbing Antoni Robinson in what can only be described as a frenzied attack. To him, it appeared that Harding had 'gone crazy'.[14]

Ashleigh Robinson

Despite the texts which Ashleigh Robinson had sent that night, she claimed she had no knowledge of what was going to happen. In fact, hours before her father's death she had sent a text to her mother, Joanne Barr:

"Im going to kill him!!!!!"[15]

On the night of the murder, Ashleigh and her sister, Holly, were in a bedroom with their boyfriends, Sacha Roberts and Gordon Harding. According to Ashleigh, the men left the bedroom, with Roberts carrying a commando-style knife, while Harding had a smaller kitchen knife.

Ashleigh told police that as far as she was aware, the two men were going to search the safe in their father's bedroom and that she had no idea her father was going to be killed, or even injured.

She locked the bedroom door with herself, her baby daughter, and her younger sister inside.

When Sacha Roberts returned to the girls' bedroom, according to Ashleigh he put his hands over her younger sister's ears and led her outside. Ashleigh followed with her baby but had to return to the bungalow for some clothes for her daughter, which is when she said she pushed open the door to her father's bedroom.

"Gordon had my dad in his arms and he was picking him up off the floor."

Harding shouted at Ashleigh to get out of the bedroom, and then followed her out. According to her, her boyfriend told her that her father was dead. But Harding later claimed that she had asked him:

"Is he dead?"

Ashleigh called her mother, Joanne Barr, and later told police that her mother had told her to lie to them, saying that Holly Robinson and Sacha Roberts had not been in the bungalow at the time of the murder. She was also told to say that she had gone into her father's bedroom with Gordon Harding and that her father had threatened them both.[16]

Holly Robinson

Holly was just 16 when her father was murdered, the baby of the family. And yet, along with her older sister and their boyfriends, she plotted the demise of the man who had raised her until a few months prior to his death. She might have got away with it, pleading her innocence, if she hadn't engaged in the text conversation which exposed her as a cold-blooded accomplice.

The Trial

The trial began on Monday, January 17th, 2011, at Mold Crown Court, in North Wales. At first, Holly was not named in the press because of her age – news reports only referred to her as 'a 16-year-old girl'. However, the judge later lifted these restrictions, meaning that Holly's identity could be released.

All four were charged with murder, despite it being likely that it was only Gordon Harding who actually stabbed Antoni Robinson. They were also charged with perverting the course of justice, along with the girls' mother, Joanne Barr, for providing a false alibi for Holly and Sacha.

Andrew Thomas QC said in his opening statement for the prosecution that Antoni Robinson had not put up a fight, contrary to Gordon Harding's claims that he acted in self-defence when Antoni 'lunged at him with a knife'. In fact, apart from the body and blood, there were no other signs of a disturbance – no ornaments were out of place, and nothing was broken, as would be expected following a violent altercation between two men. Given the appearance of the room and the positioning of the wounds on Antoni's body, it appeared that he had been 'totally overpowered' by his assailant.

Mr Thomas went on to say:

"The dreadful fact is that the persons responsible for the killing are the deceased's own daughter Ashleigh, her boyfriend Gordon Harding, a girl of 16, and another young man Sacha Roberts.

This killing was the tragic result of family disputes over money, jewellery and property. The dispute reached boiling point on the night of the fatal attack, when the defendants met up at the house.

They waited until Mr Robinson was asleep, then one or more of them entered his bedroom.

Not even the ornaments on the bedside table had been disturbed. He must have been completely overpowered."

On January 25th, 2011, 20-year-old Gordon Harding took the stand. He claimed that he had only wanted to look in the safe, but that he had been paralyzed by fear when Antoni Robinson had woken up. He was asked about the text he had sent to his co-defendant, Sacha Roberts, in which he said:

"He goes tonight, Need your backup. Ready when you are".

His reasoning for that text was that he wanted to see if there was any jewelry in the safe, jewelry which the family believed Antoni had sold. But he alleged that Antoni picked up a knife and attacked him.

Although the prosecution suspected that Antoni may have had more than one assailant, when questioned, Gordon Harding said he acted alone. He was asked if anyone else was in the room when he attacked Antoni Robinson, and he replied:

"*No, not to my knowledge.*"

Questioning continued, with Harding being asked if he was responsible for all of the wounds found on Antoni's body.

"I accept that I must have, but I don't recall causing any more than three or four wounds."

The court also heard how, in police interviews, Gordon Harding had claimed he had lost control. In court, he stated:

"It's just that I was panicking...It's just that I was terrified at what was happening."

Sacha Roberts took the stand three days later, on January 28th, 2011. He claimed that he had brought the commando-style knife with him in jest.

"I thought, should I take this as a joke? It was not anything serious. I didn't even think anything about it."

He denied ever encouraging Gordon Harding to kill Antoni Robinson and said he had never been in Mr Robinson's bedroom. He said that, as he stood on the landing, Gordon Harding had taken the knife from him, to which he was asked whether he had brought the knife with the intention of harming or killing Antoni. Again, this was denied. In fact, according to Sacha Roberts, he did not even know whether Antoni Robinson would even be in the house that night.

On Friday, February 4th, 2011, Gordon Harding and Ashleigh Robinson were found guilty of the murder of Antoni Robinson.

On Monday, February 7th, 2011, Sacha Roberts and Holly Robinson were also convicted of his murder.

In summing up, Andrew Thomas QC stated:

"This killing was the tragic result of family disputes over money, jewellery and property. The dispute reached boiling point on the night of the fatal attack when the defendants met up at the bungalow."

He went on to say that, despite Harding being the only one to inflict the wounds, and ultimately killing Antoni Robinson, the other three defendants were guilty of murder because they egged him on, and supported him in his actions. Even though Harding was the only one who entered Antoni's room that night, all four of them were in the house, and they all knew that Harding had a knife and would, more than likely, use it.

Sentencing

The four defendants were all sentenced on Tuesday, February 8th, 2011. Mr Justice Griffith Williams handed down their sentences, after labelling the girls *"Judas-like and wicked"*.

He told them:

"Antoni Robinson was murdered in his own bedroom, stabbed 15 times...you were after the jewellery in the safe...it is to be hoped that in his dying moments he was at least spared the awful realisation that it was

his own two daughters who were party to his murder...two daughters who were, in fact, scornful of him. Two daughters who had appealed for his kindness...two daughters who, Judas-like, wormed their way back into his affections."

All four of the defendants were handed life sentences, with minimum terms attached. Ashleigh Robinson and Gordon Harding were sentenced to at least 22 years, Sacha Roberts was sentenced to 20 years, and Holly Robinson was detained at her majesty's pleasure for a minimum of 18 years. Only the younger sister showed any emotion as the sentences were handed down, sobbing as she heard her fate. Sacha Roberts merely nodded at the judge, while Ashleigh Robinson and Gordon Harding remained impassive.

Joanne Barr received a four-year prison sentence for her part in the aftermath of the murder.

Following sentencing, Claire Robinson, Antoni's eldest daughter from his first marriage, read out a statement in which she paid tribute to her father.

"As a family we have waited patiently to see these heartless individuals become accountable for their crimes. Today is that day and justice has been done. My dad was a kind and loving father, brother, uncle and grandfather and we have all been deeply affected and devastated by his death. It has been proved today, without a shadow of a doubt, that our dad did nothing to provoke this and did not deserve to have his life taken so cruelly. What has made it a lot more difficult is the fact it was done by relatives who we thought we knew. It has been heart-breaking for us all to sit and hear the lies in court."[17]

Joint Enterprise

Following her release from prison, Joanne Barr joined forces with screenwriter Jimmy McGovern to hand a petition to 10 Downing Street, opposing the joint enterprise law, the law which saw her daughters jailed for life despite them not having even been in the room when their father was killed.

Joint enterprise states that anyone who is part of a group which commits a crime can be held accountable for that crime and sentenced accordingly.

The petition gained 10,000 signatures.

Joanne Barr also disputed her own conviction for perverting the course of justice, saying that she was convicted and jailed for telling the truth.

"Originally, I said my youngest daughter (Hollie) and her boyfriend weren't there. So I went back the next day and told the truth but they convicted me anyway."

She served half of her four-year sentence and was released on licence for the rest of her term. Despite the incriminating text messages which were sent on the night of the murder, Joanne Barr maintains that her daughters are innocent.

"None of us are Mystic Meg. How can any of us foresee anyone else's actions? The law is 300 years old. How can you stop someone if you don't know what is happening?"

She went on:

"We know there's a victim. But using joint enterprise, it tears us apart. I can't put it into words - I live with it daily. Until the day I die, the fight goes on. I used to be a staunch supporter of the legal system but, until you go through something like this, you don't realise how the system works. If I thought for one minute, or if they told me they had done it, I would be the first in line to say you have to do your time."[[18]

All four defendants attempted to get their sentences reduced, their lawyers claiming that the minimum terms set out in the original sentencing were too high.

Their appeals were denied, and, for now, at least, the four of them will remain behind bars.

LEE ANN REIDEL

LARRY SHERMAN

29

What could lead a normal middle class woman to be accused of killing an innocent man? This is the story of convicted murderer Lee Ann Reidel.

Early Years

Lee Ann Reidel, then Lee Ann Armanini, was born in the summer of 1967. Her childhood was very normal. She was the second of four children, to parents David and Pat Armanini. The family lived in a middle class, suburban area in Long Island, New York. Things went well for a few years; they went on regular vacations and spent the holidays together, life was good.

It was when Lee Ann turned 11 that things started to go wrong. Her parents divorced. Pat Armanini, Lee Ann's mother, moved to Florida to live with a new female lover. Lee Ann was left behind in New York. From that point she was raised by her father, David Armanini, who later remarried. Unsurprisingly, these difficult circumstances seemed to have a negative effect on Lee Ann's life and she entered a downward spiral.

Her teenage years were troubled, culminating in a failed marriage at the young age of 19. As a result of this marriage Lee Ann had her first child, a son named Christopher. Lee Ann raised Christopher alone and had the typical struggles of a young, single mother. The main worry was money; some claim that financial insecurities during this period of Lee Ann's life affected her later actions. However, despite some tough times, David Armanini, Lee Ann's father, claims that she was a responsible mother, who put the needs of her son first.

Family Life

The following years passed without incident. Lee Ann didn't have another serious boyfriend until she met Paul Reidel in 1998. The pair met at a Long Island gym where Lee Ann had started working out. They quickly fell in love. Friends of Lee Ann claim that she was very happy. She liked Paul Reidel because he was a strong, muscly man who could protect her, but he also had a gentle nature. The relationship progressed quickly, and soon they were engaged. Cathy Armanini, Lee Ann's stepmother, stated that the family were very pleased when they discovered that the pair had plans to marry.

Paul Reidel had a difficult past – he spent several years in prison on drug dealing charges when he was 19. However, he had since reformed and become a very ambitious man. He opened a business named Dolphin Fitness Club, with his best friend, Alex Algeri. Dolphin Fitness Club in Amityville, New York, was a popular 24 hour gym for weightlifters. The business was thriving and Paul was doing very well financially. Lee Ann appreciated her new lifestyle – she had gone from being a struggling single mother, to the partner of a rich business owner.

Lee Ann and Paul had a church wedding in July 1998. The wedding was quite a lavish display, with impressive decorations and catering. Guests described it as a beautiful fairy tale wedding. No one would ever have predicted the terrible events that were soon to follow.

Marriage Troubles

Not long after they were married, Lee Ann discovered that she was pregnant with her second child. Again, family members were delighted. From the outside everything seemed perfect. However, the stress of owning a 24 hour business and the prospect of being a father was starting to get to Paul. He had started using drugs again and quickly became addicted to crack cocaine.

Pat Armanini, Lee Ann's mother, claims that Lee Ann confided in her about Reidel's drug use and that she was very distressed by it. A number of incidents took place involving Lee Ann driving around during the night, trying to locate Paul and bring him back home. Pat Armanini stated that on one occasion Lee Ann even followed him to the location of a drug deal in order to prevent it from happening. This all happened while Lee Ann was heavily pregnant. Lee Ann wanted to preserve their relationship and help Paul get off drugs. Her mother believes that she thought the new baby would fix things between them, and be the wake-up call that Paul needed to stop taking crack cocaine.

For a short time, this did seem to be the case. Paul became very excited about the idea of having a child, especially when he found out it was a boy. When the child was born, they called him Nicholas. Paul asked his best friend and business partner, Alex Algeri, to be Nicholas' godfather. Algeri happily agreed.

However, despite a happy period, Paul Reidel's drugs habits remained. He continued to use crack cocaine regularly. Lee Ann would apparently find needles and vials around the house, and feared that their small child would end up getting injured or worse. In July 2000, things came to ahead and Paul returned home from work one night to find that Lee Ann, his new born baby and stepson, were gone. Also missing was a large amount of money and possessions from the house. Lee Ann had fled to her mother's place in Florida with the children, taking $120000 with her.

Losing his family seemed to be the wake-up call that Paul Reidel needed. He was afraid that he would no longer be able to see his son. Reidel hired a lawyer to help fight for shared custody of Nicholas and he wanted Lee Ann and the baby to come back to New York while they waited for a custody decision. Paul stated that he wanted to be part of Nicholas' life, and he couldn't do that from so far away. Ultimately though, Reidel did not want his family to fall apart and he spent the next four months trying to reconcile with his wife. He made many promises to Lee Ann during this time. Most importantly, Reidel agreed to go to rehab and ditch his cocaine habit.

Lee Ann and the children eventually returned to Long Island in December 2000. It seemed like the two were trying to sort out their marriage and wanted to try again. Everyone believed that they had gotten over the difficult drugs issues and were now on the path towards happy family life once more. Paul was pleased, he was able to stay in the area of his business, and see his wife and son every day. However, not all was as it seemed and Lee Ann's motivations for returning to Long Island would later be called into question.

The Murder

One month later on the 17th January 2001, an unbelievable act of violence took place. Alex Algeri was shot in the face and killed outside the Dolphin Fitness Club. Gym members and the local community of Amityville were shocked; it was obviously a cold blooded murder.

Like any typical January in New York, the weather was very cold and there was a covering of snow on the ground. It was 7.20 in the evening and already dark. It was Paul Reidel's night off; Alex Algeri was covering the late shift at the gym. During what had so far been a perfectly normal evening, Alex popped out to get a CD from his car for one of the regular aerobics classes. He exited the building through the backdoor. The car park was not well lit and would have been very dark. He went round to the passenger side of the car to collect the CD from the glove compartment. Suddenly, a man jumped out of another vehicle parked nearby. As Algeri turned around, the man shot him several times in the face and neck.

Alex Algeri made it back into the gym trying to get help, but quickly collapsed and was dead before he arrived at hospital.

There was chaos. No one could understand why anyone would want Alex Algeri dead. The consensus was that Algeri was a friendly, popular individual who didn't have any known enemies. For a long time, the police had no leads in their investigation into the murder and people began to wonder if Algeri was really the intended victim.

Rumours spread that perhaps the killer had meant to shoot Paul Reidel instead. After all, Paul was the one with the criminal background. He had taken and dealt drugs for many years, and could have gotten involved with the wrong person. Maybe he had drug related debts, or someone was jealous of his flashy lifestyle. However, at this point there was no evidence that this was the case.

Lee Ann seemed to become panicked after Algeri's funeral. She apparently started asking Paul if it was supposed to be him, and what if she and the baby had been there – what if someone came to their house. Lee Ann convinced Paul that they might be in danger in New York, and that the family should move back to Florida.

Running Away

In 2001, the family did just this. Reidel, Lee Ann and the two children, Christopher and Nicholas, moved back to Florida permanently. Reidel was now the sole owner of the Dolphin Fitness Club and he wanted to remain in charge of the Long Island business. He decided to try and run things from Florida, flying out on regular business trips to check how everything was going. Lee Ann and Paul had plans to build a house for them and their two children in Florida. According to Lee Ann's friend, Mary Hanrahan, Lee Ann and Reidel were both very positive about the move. Reidel apparently spoke excitedly about their plans to build a property and yet again, everything appeared to be going fine for them.

The police in Long Island still had a murder investigation with no leads. Months passed without any new information on the case.

On one of Paul's many business trips to New York he received some unpleasant news from a relative. His relative claimed that every time Paul went out of town, a man went to see Lee Ann at the husband and wife's apartment in Florida. The suspicion was that Lee Ann was involved in an affair.

Reidel quickly dismissed the stories about Lee Ann being unfaithful. He believed that their relationship was stronger than ever because Lee Ann was pregnant again. He even told his relatives that the couple planned to call their new baby Paul, after him. Perhaps some family members had their doubts, but for several months everything went smoothly and Lee Ann and Reidel seemed content together.

A Lead

However, all that was about to change. In November 2001 police arrested a drug dealer in New York, named Michael Hubbard. Hubbard tipped off police that Ralph Salierno and Scott Paget from Florida were involved in the murder of Alex Algeri. Hubbard was trying to help the police and give them the impression that he was cooperating in the hope that his own drug dealing convictions would be dropped.

Police quickly brought in Salierno and Paget for questioning. From the very beginning Paget claimed that Salierno was the one who actually committed the murder and fired the gun at Algeri. Paget stated that he was just the driver. Salierno feigned ignorance about the murder for a while, but when he discovered that Paget had pointed the finger at him, he decided to offer his own rundown of events. In Salierno's story, Lee Ann was the one who came up with the plan to commit a murder, and Salierno was merely trying to follow her instructions.

Salierno confirmed that he and Lee Ann had been having an affair since the first time she moved to Florida in July 2000. Lee Ann's own mother, Pat Armanini, had introduced them, with the idea that Salierno could protect Lee Ann if Paul Reidel ever came to Florida and tried to take baby Nicholas. However, the relationship had developed into something much more. The two had fallen in love and kept seeing each other even when Lee Ann and Reidel were supposedly back together. Salierno claimed that Lee Ann had given him instructions to go to New York and kill Paul Reidel, offering him a potential payment of $100000. Salierno said that the killing of Alex Algeri was a case of mistaken identity.

Paul Reidel and Alex Algeri did not look dissimilar; they were both very strong, muscular men and had similar features. Obviously, they shared the same work place and even drove the same type of car. The murder had also taken place in the poorly lit gym carpark on a dark January evening. A case of mistaken identity did not seem impossible to police. Salierno's story was further backed up when he revealed that he was the father of Lee Ann's third child. This proved to be true, meaning that Lee Ann and Salierno had continued to see each other even after Alex Algeri's murder. So far, Salierno's version of events appeared to be adding up.

After Salierno admitted to killing Alex Algeri, Lee Ann confessed that she had indeed been having an affair with Salierno. The new baby, named Zachary, was his. However, she strongly denied that she had any part in planning her husband's murder. Lee Ann claimed that Salierno must have committed the murder in a fit of jealousy over the fact that the husband and wife appeared to be reconciling, and that Algeri was simply in the wrong place at the wrong time. Lee Ann also said that she had continued the affair with Salierno after Alex Algeri's death because her husband had changed – he was withdrawn and paranoid. She maintained that she had no idea that Salierno was the one who killed Algeri.

The police were put in a difficult situation – they were faced with numerous conflicting stories and very little physical evidence. They concluded that the only option was to let the case go to court and see what the outcome would be. In March 2003 Lee Ann Reidel was also arrested for the murder of Alex Algeri, it was decided that she and Salierno would be co-defendants.

The Trial

In March 2004, Lee Ann and Salierno were tried in the same room at Suffolk County courthouse, and faced the same prosecutors, but the outcome would be decided by two different juries. This is quite an unusual set up. The pair faced several charges including first degree murder, second degree murder and conspiracy to commit murder.

The prosecutor was Assistant District Attorney Denise Merrifield. Merrifield began by establishing that the intended victim was in fact, Paul Reidel, not Alex Algeri. Salierno confirmed this in his admission. The real question was did Salierno act alone, or was he acting on the instruction of Lee Ann?

Many witnesses were called upon during the trial. There was no physical evidence of Lee Ann's involvement so the prosecution relied heavily on the testimony of these witnesses. One notable testimony was from Lee Ann's mother's former lover, Elizabeth Russo. Russo claimed that she and Lee Ann's mother had initially introduced Lee Ann and Salierno with the intention of providing protection to Lee Ann. Salierno was told that if Paul Reidel came to Florida Salierno should threaten him and break his legs. This account suggested that Lee Ann was open to violent acts towards Paul Reidel. Russo clearly implied that she believed Lee Ann was capable of giving the instruction to Salierno to commit murder. Russo's account was particularly important for the prosecution because, unlike most of the other witnesses they called, she was not a criminal.

Scott Paget had already admitted that he drove Salierno back and forth to Long Island, New York on the night of the murder. Paget said that Salierno paid him $3000 dollars to drive the getaway car. He received a lower sentence of 18 years for cooperation with police. He also testified against Lee Ann – though the defence maintained that he could have simply been doing this in order to help his own case. Paget testified that Lee Ann instructed Salierno to kill Reidel. He said that Lee Ann gave Salierno a photograph of Reidel and told him the address of the Dolphin Fitness Club. Although this was a damning testimony, the defence tried to argue that Paget was not a reliable witness due to his own conviction and involvement in the case.

However, Lee Ann's case was damaged further when Michael Paglianti, a Florida drug dealer, was called to give his testimony. He said that he had been present when Lee Ann and Salierno met and discussed breaking Paul Reidel's legs. He also claimed that he had heard Lee Ann say that she wanted Reidel dead. Paglianti corroborated Paget's story by saying that he saw Lee Ann give a photograph of Reidel to Salierno. Finally, Paglianti testified that after the night of the murder and Algeri's funeral, Lee Ann verbally abused Salierno for killing the wrong guy.

Having heard from numerous witnesses, Lee Ann's case was not looking good. However, the defence pointed out that most of the witnesses were criminals and there was still no physical evidence of Lee Ann's guilt. There were some discrepancies with the car that Salierno and Paget drove to Long Island, with no record of who paid for the car, or where they rented it from. Lee Ann's attorney, Bruce Barket, questioned why Salierno had killed the wrong man. Surely, if he was acting on Lee Ann's instruction, he would have known that it was Reidel's night off and that Algeri was working at the club that night.

There was still the question of why Lee Ann would want her husband dead. The prosecution had a simple answer for this – money. They claimed that Lee Ann wanted Paul Reidel out of the picture so that she could start a new life with Salierno whilst living comfortably on Reidel's savings.

The prosecution, Denise Merrifield, believed that Lee Ann already started developing the plan to murder Reidel the first time she was in Florida in July 2000. Merrifield suggested that Lee Ann knew that if the husband and wife remained separated when Reidel was killed, she would be a number one suspect. Merrifield said that Lee Ann then pretended to reconcile with Reidel and moved back to New York, all whilst plotting his murder with Salierno. Her plan was to act like the grieving widow after his death, in order to seem innocent. As Reidel's wife, his fortune would be left to her and she would let some time pass before quietly moving back to Florida to be with Salierno.

Of course, the defence disputed this story. Defence attorney Bruce Barket maintained that Salierno went to New York in a fit of rage upon seeing that Lee Ann and Reidel were back together. Barket stated that Salierno's actions were irrational and not well planned; this is how he ended up shooting the wrong person. According to the defence, Lee Ann was oblivious to the fact that Salierno had killed Algeri and that her only wrong doing was the ongoing affair with Salierno.

In the end, it seemed like the decision could go either way for Lee Ann.

The Decision

The jury deciding the fate of Salierno returned to the court room in just four hours. He was found guilty of first degree murder and Judge Louis Ohlig sentenced him to life in prison with no parole.

Lee Ann's jury took longer to reach a decision. Her defence attorney believed that this was a good sign for her case. However, after four long days, the jury found her guilty too. Lee Ann was held equally responsible for the death of Alex Algeri. On the 28th April 2004, she was sentenced to twenty five years to life. The prosecution did not ask for life without parole for Lee Ann. They did not give any comment on why this was, which was unusual because the judge even stated that he would have happily given a longer sentence to Lee Ann had the prosecution asked for it.

Prosecutor Merrifield told the judge that "Justice has been served here, your honour. She, because of her own greed and evil heart, wanted her husband dead. This defendant is the most self-absorbed defendant I have ever prosecuted."

Bruce Barket, Lee Ann's defence attorney, was very upset by the outcome of the case. This is clear from his response to the decision: "I respect the Jury system. I respect the Jury process. I strongly disagree with the verdict."

Although Lee Ann's attorney claims to respect the Jury process, there has been some criticism of the way the case was handled in court. Some believe that the fact that Lee Ann and Salierno were tried in the same room was actually damaging to Lee Ann's case. The psychology of seeing the pair together, with the knowledge that they had an ongoing affair and a child together, could have affected the Jury's decision. The idea that Lee Ann was guilty of something was already in the minds of the Jury members, perhaps they found it hard to make an objective decision on Lee Ann's guilt in relation to the murder itself.

There was also the fact that the unintended victim of the murder was someone completely innocent and well liked. This caused wide spread anger, even those who did not know Alex Algeri felt that it was a real tragedy and an injustice. People were calling for the death penalty, though this was not requested by the prosecution. The high levels of emotion and anger surrounding the case could also have impacted on the Jury's decision making. It's hard to say if the reaction would have been the same if Reidel had been the one killed. It is possible that it would have been easier for the defence to portray Reidel as someone involved in a criminal lifestyle and Lee Ann as a fearful wife, desperate to escape his control. As Algeri was the victim, the Judge potentially felt a lot of pressure to dish out harsh sentences in an attempt to restore justice.

Alex Algeri was only 32 when he was murdered. His sister, Christie Stoll, told the judge "our brother is gone and the hole in our hearts will never be filled because of [Lee Ann's] greed and hatred of her husband. Even though Lee Ann Reidel wasn't there on the night of January 17th 2001, she just as well might have been. Lee Ann Reidel is just as guilty as Ralph Salierno." After the trial Algeri's father, Salvatore Algeri, said that "justice has been served completely."

Despite the defence claiming no evidence, and the issue raised about the nature of the trial, the widely held opinion is that justice was done and that Lee Ann was guilty for her part in Alex Algeri's murder.

Zachary, Lee Ann's third child, fathered by Salierno, is living with Lee Ann's sister in Long Island. Lee Ann and Reidel's son Nicholas is living with Reidel and no longer has any contact with his mother. Paul Reidel gave an insightful interview on the extremely popular talk show, Larry King live. He said that Lee Ann wanted him dead because she knew he would never stop fighting for access to their son. When asked if he felt lucky to have avoided murder, Reidel said "I don't feel lucky, because I would have took that walk. I would have never asked him to do it, and whatever happened, that's a burden I'll always carry." Reidel explained that his life is in order and his ongoing focus is raising his son. "I feel like I have a severe obligation to be a good man and do the right thing by my son because I feel like I owe that to Alex". King also asked Reidel what his feelings were towards Lee Ann, Reidel said that he did not hate her, but that he was confused and that he felt that she deserved the prison sentence.

Salierno is currently serving his sentence at Attica Correctional Facility in New York. Lee Ann is at Bedford Hills Correctional Facility also in New York. So far, her attempts to appeal have been unsuccessful.

SHE KILLED THE PREACHER

John Fontaine

The Case of Mary Winkler

Mary Winkler, at first appearances, would seem to be an altogether normal woman. So too did her family, with a husband who was a Church minister and three young children, girls aged just eight, six and one.

The family lived in Selmer, Tenn., a small town occupied by around 4,500 people, according to the 2015 census. The town is situated to the south west of the state. Not much has happened in Selmer; the most famous person to have been born there was Chad Harville, former pitcher for the Oakland A's, and for one year, the Red Sox. He achieved a 4-9 win-loss record over his career in the MLB.

Today, the most famous- or infamous- person to have come from Selmer is Mary Winkler. In 2006, Mary sparked a border-crossing manhunt, and a court case followed nationwide. She had killed her husband with a shot to the back from the family's shotgun. But it was the gripping, and at times bizarre, court case which gripped the attention of the nation.

Matthew dead, Mary and the family Missing

The date was March 6th, 2007. It was a Tuesday like any other. Mary and Matthew were at home all day together, although Matthew was due to give a sermon that evening.

It was actually members of Matthew's congregation who found his body that night. They had visited his home to check up on him after he had missed the service he was set to give; instead, they found him lying dead, having been shot in the back.

There was no sign of Mary or any of their children at the home, and as such, they were reported missing. The authorities quickly sent out an Amber Alert, since nobody had any idea what could have happened to them, or where they might be. Family and friends had no information to provide police on their whereabouts.

There was every chance that the family had been kidnapped or murdered, and their bodies disposed of elsewhere, although police could not identify a break in, and had no reason to believe that anything of value had been stolen.

It was only a day later that she was arrested in Alabama, having run from the family home with her young children. They were found 350 miles away from home, at Orange Beach, and in the back seat of the van was the family's shotgun. It was certainly suspicious; but what reason could Mary have possibly had for committing such a crime?

The Trial

In the build up to the case going to trial, public interest ramped up. Speculation had been rife about why Mary would have murdered her husband, a seemingly nice, well respected member of the local community. Perhaps either one of them had had an affair, and Matthew had been killed in a crime of passion. Or maybe he had been killed for an insurance claim?

As such, the press reported every step of the story as it came out during the hearing. The trial began when a Tennessee Bureau of Investigation Agent John Mehr read a statement that Mary had made very soon after her arrest. In it, Mary claimed that the couple had been arguing about their family finances, before Mary had shot her husband with their 12 gauge shotgun. She had said that the last thing she had wanted was to actually murder her husband, but she had been brandishing the gun in an effort to convince him to work through their problems, together. The argument had been ongoing throughout the day, and Mary had finally snapped, resorting to drastic measures to be able to convince him. She had never intended to kill him: she had said in the statement, 'I don't want this at all. I don't want any of this to be, at all.'

The statement continued on, and Mary claimed that they had argued often and argued fiercely. 'He had really been on me lately,' Mary had said, 'criticizing me for things- the way I walk, I eat, everything. It was just building up to a point. I was tired of it. I guess I got to a point and snapped.'

At first glance, it would seem that Mary had simply lost her composure, become angry, and killed her husband 'as the red mist had descended'. But after their initial statement, Mary's attorney indicated that there was much more that would come out about Matthew's behaviour when she testified which would help to explain her actions. Clearly, there were more problems with their marriage than the occasional, albeit fierce, argument.

Mary's Crime

The case for the prosecution wasted no time in painting Mary as a cold blooded killer, who left her husband to die without remorse. Admittedly, the plain facts of the case made Mary seem unbelievably guilty. The prosecution relied on several of these facts in their attempt to convince the jury of Mary's guilt for the charge of murder.

Mary had disconnected the phone immediately after she shot her husband, stopping him from being able to call the emergency services, or receive any calls that may have come in. This suggested that Mary had been in full control of her actions, not panicking, since it is unlikely that somebody in a state of anxiety would think to disconnect the phone.

The fact that Mary had attempted to flee to Orange Beach, Alabama, was also a key point for the prosecution. Immediately after Matthew's death, Mary had taken the family minivan to the beach, with her three children. Later on in her defence, Mary would claim that she ran because '[n]obody would believe me, and they'd take the girls away and put me away.' Certainly, in many murder cases, the fact that the defendant flees the scene is a certain indicator of guilt.

The family's daughter Patricia testified that she couldn't understand her mother's actions. All that she knew was that she had heard a 'big boom', and the sound of something heavy hitting the floor. She quickly ran to the bedroom to see her father on the floor, and her mother holding the shotgun. She had no idea what could possibly have provoked her mother to shoot him.

Another sticking point was that the family finances had been 'in shambles' just before the murder had taken place. This had led Mary to become embroiled in what is called a 'check kiting' scam. In it, she had received checks from unidentified accounts in Canada and Nigeria, and had ultimately fallen to a financial scam that had lost the family money. Prosecutors claimed that this could have somehow instigated the argument that led to Matthew's death, and that Mary had felt as if she had no way out of the scam.

They also jumped on the fact that in an initial conversation with investigators, Mary had told them that their marriage was a happy one, and that '[t]here's no poor me. I'm in control.' They clearly wanted to paint a picture of Mary as remorseless, deceitful, and smarter than she looked.

The Cross-examination

During her cross-examination in court, Mary stated that she didn't remember grabbing the gun from the closet in which it was kept. What she did remember was that 'something went off', 'hearing a loud boom', and that 'it wasn't as loud as I thought it would be.' She did admit that she had shot her husband. Matthew rolled from the bed- upon which he had been lying as they had argued- and dropped to the floor. Mary described smelling gunpowder.

Prosecutor Walter Freeland asked her whether she understood that 'pulling a trigger is what makes it go boom', to which she replied that she did.

Matthew asked her why she had snapped and shot him. She could only say 'I'm sorry.' The shotgun blast had been inflicted from behind, directly into Matthew's back, and had caused severe damage to his organs and spine. According to prosecutors, he had in fact still been alive as Mary had run from the house.

But these simple facts were far from the end of the story, as Mary was to reveal.

Appearances and Revelations

At first, Mary spoke of her husband not in the past tense, but in the present, as if she couldn't quite understand how final her actions really had been. In reminiscing about happier times, Mary told the court that her husband was an intelligent, social man, and that the family had shared many 'good times' together. She also seemed to enjoy talking about her children, and the happiness they brought her.

This happy family life, however, was simply one side of the marriage. Mary's attorney stated that '[w]hat went on behind their closed doors is going to have to be told ... Some of what we've got from the state of Tennessee touches on sexual abuse.' Their defence was that Matthew had made Mary's life a 'living hell': '[w]e will show you proof that he would destroy objects that she loved, he would isolate her from her family and he would abuse her not just verbally, not just emotional and not just physically—in other ways, too.'

Just before the murder, Mary claimed that Matthew had been threatening their children and even attempted to throttle their infant daughter, Breanna. He had been shouting, angry, because he had wanted a son. As the case went on, it became obvious that this was only the tip of the iceberg, however, and more and more sordid details of their home life would come to light.

Matthew, Mary claimed, was a violent, abusive husband. Shortly after their marriage, he ordered her to stop socialising with any of her family and friends (a common tactic among abusive spouses in order to further isolate their partners from potential help). Winkler's sisters described how Mary seemed stuck in her marriage, unhappy, but unable to leave. In an interview, they said that 'As the years went on, she seemed to be nervous to show love towards us.'

Mary was commonly 'screamed and hollered' at by her husband. 'He just flailed. He's a big guy and he was just all over ... He'd point his finger inches away from my nose. Whatever he was upset about, it was my fault,' Mary had said. It could be over anything: 'I was fat, my hair wasn't right, the girls, if something went wrong, it was my fault. I didn't know when it was coming.' Mary described her situation as one familiar to abused wives and husbands across America.

Her attorney, Steve Farese, provided further information based on his conversations with Mary. She had needed her husband's permission for everything, even for getting her hair cut. 'This was constant, and she lived a life where she walked on eggshells.' This abuse, he said, had given Mary symptoms of post traumatic stress disorder, simply because 'she didn't know what was going to happen next.' Furthermore, a psychologist testified as part of Mary's defence, saying that her symptoms were those of clinical depression and PTSD.

During her time on the stand, Mary also claimed that Matthew had forced her to watch pornography with him, and that he had bought her several 'slutty' costumes for sex, which she normally would never have worn, but for fear of her husband. If she refused, Matthew wouldn't hesitate to get physical, hitting her or even using his belt to whip her. Mary famously produced a wig and a pair of white high heels in the witness box during her cross-examination to show the court evidence of Matthew's other side.

Mary stated that she was never happy watching pornography, dressing up in sexy outfits or performing the sex acts that Matthew wanted. She went along with his ideas, however, because she didn't dare face his reaction if she didn't. 'I'd just do anything to help him stay happy.' Throughout these revelations, Mary was visibly embarrassed and uncomfortable. Clearly she would have preferred that none of them had ever come to light; but Mary felt it necessary to brave what her neighbors, and the nation, might think in order to clear her name and justify her actions.

Mary's family had been quick to corroborate her side of the story. Her father, Clark Freeman, had spoken out through Good Morning America and detailed the 'physical, mental, verbal' abuse that his daughter had suffered. Other friends came forward during the court case, and gave similar verdicts on their relationship. A friend of Mary's,

Rudie Thomsen, said that '[o]ne Sunday, Mary came into the church and I looked at her and she had a black eye.' Similarly, Mary's friend Amy Redmon agreed that Matthew had been controlling: '[h]e was an authority figure, and he made the decisions basically. It was obvious.'

Conversely, Matthew's family denied that their son had been anything like Mary had depicted in her defence testimony. Matthew's father, Charles Daniel Winkler, said that his son was a kind, gentle man, who could have done nothing to justify what the defence was claiming. Diane spoke several times during the trial, lashing out at Mary: 'You've never told your girls you're sorry! Don't you think you at least owe them that?'

The dramatic story of a supposedly kindly, gentle church minister having such a sordid, cruel and abusive hidden life gripped America. The case was covered extensively on all major networks, discussed on late night panel shows

The Jury's Verdict

While the prosecutors had tried to convince the jury to convict her on a charge of first degree murder, they were unsuccessful. The jury came to their verdict by April, that year. It took them eight hours to deliberate their way to the decision; this mirrored the response of the nation, which was similarly undecided on just what punishment Mary really deserved.

Mary was found guilty of voluntary manslaughter, a charge which carries a far more lenient sentence than murder. While murderers can receive full life sentences, and in certain states receive the death penalty, the maximum sentence for voluntary manslaughter is only 6 years.

Mary showed little emotion at the verdict, but did embrace each of her relatives afterwards. In a show of support, her family had been sat in the row behind her, and all linked arms with one another to demonstrate their solidarity. Afterwards, she was taken back into custody to await sentencing.

Mary's attorney stated afterwards that Mary's testimony had been central in securing the more lenient sentence. 'I think Mary's testimony was integral in this decision. They had to hear it from Mary', Farese told the press. 'They judged her credibility and they saw that she had an abusive relationship and they made their judgment based upon that.'

For Mary, the most important implication of the verdict was that she could finally begin to think of being reunited with her children. Speaking on her behalf after the trial, Farese continued: 'We would like to do so many things to open up communication between Mary and the paternal grandparents and to get the children out of this cycle of constant upheaval over this terrible tragic event.' But the question of how long she would be in prison remained.

Mary's sentencing was scheduled for May 18th, at which point both Mary and the prosecution would have a final chance to address the court before the judge decided on the final jail term. However, the situation looked positive for Mary. Not only would the five months that she had been imprisoned awaiting trial be taken into consideration, but the judge had indicated that alternatives to incarceration would be on the table. Perhaps Mary could avoid jail time altogether.

Sentencing: The Trial at an End

Due to a scheduling error, the hearing took place around three weeks late, on June 8th.

Mary took to the stand one last time to plead for mercy. She read aloud from a prepared statement, telling Matthew's family of her sorrow and remorse for her actions. She was 'so sorry that this had happened', and would 'always miss and love' her husband. 'I ask for mercy and understanding, but I know whatever decision you reach today will be right ... I ask you to please let me go home today and be with my children.' Tabitha Freeman- Mary's sister- had also pleaded for leniency, in particular to let Mary be reunited with her children. She went as far as calling Mary 'the best example of a good person I can think of'.

Members of Matthew's family, too, took to the stand to plead their case for the prosecution. Charles and his wife were clearly hurt and in disbelief at Mary's actions both in murdering their son, and believed that Mary had purposefully smeared his name at trial. 'The monster that you have painted for the world to see? I don't think that monster existed,' Diane Winkler had said.

After speaking their pieces, all that Mary, her family, and Matthew's parents could do was wait until the judge's decision. The trial- as well as the very public 'trial' that Mary had been through in the media- was finally at an end.

The defence had requested that Mary be granted full probation, or judicial diversion, both outcomes which would have meant that Mary would spent no further time in prison, and even that her record would be cleared of wrongdoing altogether. This request was denied.

After recess, Mary was told that she would spend 3 years in prison for her crime. But Circuit Judge J. Weber McCraw reduced that amount to just 210 days total in prison before she would be allowed to leave on probation. She also had that sentence reduced further, due to the fact that she had spent five months incarcerated waiting for trial.

Moreover, that time would be spent not in jail, but in a mental health centre in Tennessee. There, she would receive treatment for both her depression and post traumatic stress disorder. After such a long ordeal, with the prosecution fighting to either put Mary on death row or to imprison her indefinitely, it seemed that she had gotten off with hardly a slap on the wrist.

Steve Farese branded the sentence 'a victory': '[s]he could be in prison for life, and that's what everybody thought she was headed for to begin with.' Her other attorney, Leslie Ballin, said '[s]he'll be able to get out and fight the battle she wants to, and that is to get her children back.' Mary could finally think about the future again.

But certain signs indicated that it would not be as easy to reconcile with her children and family as she might hope. Matthew's family left the courtroom without making a comment to the press, as did the prosecution, clearly disappointed in the verdict. They gave no indication that they would be happy to open dialogue about Mary's daughters- not with the woman whom they believed to have murdered their son in cold blood.

The aftermath of Mary's release

Mary was released on August 14th, 2007. She had only been sentenced the previous June.

Upon her release, her lawyer informed the press that Mary would not be speaking with them, to maintain her privacy. During her time in the mental health facility, Mary could finally begin her attempt to win full custody of her three daughters, and she was still fighting this case at the time of her release. She had not seen her children, apart from Patricia's brief testimony as part of the case, for over a year. Throughout the case, and after Mary's release, her children were staying with Matthew's family.

Moreover, she was still fighting a $2 million dollar civil lawsuit filed by Matthew's parents. They also took legal measures, which, if successful, would have meant that the custody of Mary's children remained with them.

After her release, Mary seemed happier to her family and friends. From an outside perspective, it could be easy to claim that this was just as much due to her happiness at avoiding a jail sentence as it was to her being rid of an abuser. She was in fact living with friends at first after her release, and went back to work at a dry cleaners in McMinnville, Tenn., 200 miles from Selmer.

In the same interview as was mentioned before, Mary's sisters agreed that she had changed entirely. After years of shyness, Mary seeming unable or unwilling to show love to them for fear of her husband's violence, she seemed to finally be able to open up. 'Now it's back to the old Mary [who] loves us and doesn't care to come and hug us and gives us a kiss on the cheek.'

Since then, Mary lived in McMinnville. She has moved between jobs, working at the dry cleaners, before starting work at a nursery. She briefly dated the brother of one of her most vocal supporters, Paul Pillow; afterwards, she moved in with Wayne Cantrell, a preacher living in Smithville nearby.

Mary regained custody of her three children in 2008, but by 2010, received the news that she had multiple sclerosis. Her diagnosis came at the worst time, as she was settling down in her new life; she had not long started medical school with the desire to become a nurse, and had to quit since the work would be too demanding. She hasn't returned to work since.

One comfort for Mary was that Matthew's parents seemed close to being able to forgive her. After her diagnosis, they gave Mary some time off from parenting by taking care of the children for a weekend, which soon turned into several months. Daniel Winkler has preached several times since the events on the topic of forgiveness, although when asked by local press why he chose the topic, he has refused to answer, presumably preferring to keep those details private.

Mary, too, preferred to put the past behind her. In an interview with WAFF 48, the NBC affiliate in Huntsville AL., she stated how she would prefer to stay out of the limelight, particularly for the sake of her girls. 'Whatever reason people have any problem with me, that's fine. Everybody's entitled to their opinion, but these girls are treated for who they are, not because of what their mother's done ... They're three very fine young ladies'.

Concluding Thoughts

Some members of the public reacted with disgust at the abnormally short sentence that Mary was given, and questioned whether a husband would have been given the same leniency as Mary was. Men's rights activist Glenn Sacks publicly questioned whether a man would have been shown such leniency, and pointed to the case of Scott Peterson (who received the death penalty for the murder of his pregnant wife) to indicate that no, a man would not. He also argued that the idea of abuse had been widened to include simple criticism, and should therefore not necessarily be used as defence of murder.

Conversely, there have been many women put in prison for murdering their abusive husbands, some for much longer than Mary Winkler. The 'battered woman defense', or the preferred terminology today of 'battering and its effects', is not a genuine legal defence in itself; it can, however, be used to convince a court of diminished responsibility. Its effectiveness is due to the sympathy that it elicits from jurors, who can be convinced that abuse is a form of provocation, and the murder a form of self defense. Under this defense, Mary's short sentence makes sense.

The case has remained a touch stone with regards to spousal abuse in the U.S. A made-for-TV movie, 'The Pastor's Wife', was released in 2011. It was based on the book of the same title, written by Dianne Fanning, an award winning crime writer. The story was changed somewhat, with the inclusion of a financial subplot involving tax fraud. However, it also made use of real life interviews with people who knew the Winklers- including Matthew's parents. His mother revealed that she could never believe Mary's story. Charles admitted that Mary's story could be true, and that he could forgive her if she confessed her purposeful intention to murder Matthew.

As for the community in which the family had lived, the reaction was largely one of forgiveness. According to members of that community, the town's 'Christian roots and ... its tendency to give people the benefit of the doubt' meant that they took Mary at her word. Mary's quite life in McMinnville and Smithville similarly shows that the American public would rather leave her and her family alone after their painful ordeal.

TRACEY GRISSOM

Claiming to be a victim of rape and other abuses, a distraught Tracey Grissom would travel to her ex-husband Hunter's workplace and shoot him six times in the back, receiving a twenty-five-year life sentence for his murder.

Her defense attorney would argue that Tracey was motivated by post-traumatic stress disorder caused by her Hunter's constant abuse and sexual assaults. One jury member had even asked the judge to be lenient in her sentencing as they were not allowed to hear details of her Hunter's alleged abuses (beatings, rape, sodomy).

But what really happened in the years that led up to May 15th, 2012? Was she in fact the victim of years of abuse by a psychotic husband? Or did she want to cash in on his $100,000 life insurance policy?

INSTANT ATTRACTION

The couple would meet during a dinner party in 2003 in Tuscaloosa, Alabama. Tracey was twenty-one years old and going through a divorce. She had a son, James Michael, from the previous marriage.

Family and friends would describe the union as "love at first sight." Hunter was blown away by the young Tracey's blue eyes and facial beauty.

"For him, it was love at first sight," crime author William Phelps said. "She was gorgeous."

A whirlwind courtship would ensue and the couple would elope in 2004.

"In the beginning, it was good," Tracey told CBS' 48 hours. "We had a friendship. Just your normal, honeymoon phase marriage."

"He was fun," Tracey said. "And he was attractive."

Hunter was two years younger than Tracey, however, and his mother felt that he had jumped the gun too early in the relationship.

Her words proved to be prophetic as after only eight months into the marriage, the marriage went south.

According to Tracey, their marital problems began with Hunter's drug addiction.

"I had caught him smoking marijuana," Tracey said. "Doing illegal things could cause a problem and I couldn't risk losing my son over."

Tracey claimed that she threatened her new spouse with a divorce but Hunter gave her his word that he would stop with his drug use. She stated that the relationship improved and the decided to start a construction company together.

"I took out an equity line to start a company," Tracey said. "Which was Grissom Construction. It was all in my name."

Hunter specialized in building elaborate boat docks. He had an artistic eye and could do docks, stairs, and other accouterments. The business began to grow in short order.

"They're going to take on the world," Phelps said. "They're going to be entrepreneurs and they're gonna make it."

They then had a daughter of their own, Anna Grace. The child was a long time coming for the couple. They had been trying for a long time as Tracey had five miscarriages before Anna Grace was born.

"She was premature," Tracey recalled. "Her heart and lungs were not developed. A very stressful time."

Behind closed doors things were rocky. On the surface, however, things looked good. They had a young family and were making money.

"All-American family," Phelps said. "White-picket fence. The whole nine yards. Middle-class. Suburbia. Maybe the Prince Charming that she's been waiting for."

But again, this was only on the surface. Tracey harbored secrets of her own. One of which was her own addiction to prescription drugs.

"Psychologically, there's something going on here," Phelps said. "There's something going on behind those beautiful eyes and it ain't good."

Tracey would often turn on on the children, showing off her temper. Then she would turn on Hunter.

"This would cause friction in the marriage," Phelps said. "And where there's friction, there's fire."

SETTING THE STAGE

Tracey would later state that Hunter would "act strangely" shortly before she filed divorce. She was a registered nurse and gave him an over-the-counter drug test. According to her, Hunter tested posted for marijuana, Oxycontin, opiates, and methamphetamine.

Hunter would later be arrested for marijuana possession but his family would insist that he never did the harder drugs.

Tracey would file for divorce in the summer of 2010 after six years of marriage. According to her, this would prompt physical abuse from Hunter.

Hunter had to move out but their divorce agreement would allow him access to the home.

"In September of 2010," Tracey recalled. "That was the first time he physically hit me. It (the abuse) got progressively worse. He had made the comments that if I told anybody he would kill me. I believed him."

Hunter' co-workers and family members would have a different take on the situation, however. His co-workers remembered a time when she tracked him down at one of the jobs and made a scene.

"She's screaming, jumping on him," Hunter's co-worker said. "Said something about him having another girlfriend and used the expression about, 'You are mine. I'll kill you. I'll kill you. You are mine."

"She's borderline demonic," Hunter's mother said. " mean, I absolutely believe—that she is that troubled."

Hunter's family continued to believe that he did not abuse Tracey.

"He did not have an abusive, an angry bone in his body," Hunter's aunt Gina said. "In fact, we kind of laughed at him because he was too laid-back."

The divorce was finalized in October of 2010.

EVIDENCE OF ABUSE?

Loran Richards was the first of Tracey's friends to notice the minor injuries on her body. She would inquire about the bruises but the answers she received were always evasive. Seeing Tracey with a black eye, however, forced her to try and get more answers.

"I said, Tracey, you may have terrible luck," Richards recalled. "But nobody is so unlucky that they trip, fall down the stairs, and hit their face on a baseball in the eye socket. So don't give me a lame excuse. You don't have to give me any excuse, but let's take a picture."

Tracey broke down. She gave her friend all of the grisly details, detailing the abuse she suffered at the hands of Hunter. Loran then became her advocate, taking pictures of Tracey's injuries. She would later state that she saw blood stains and other signs of abuse at Tracey's home.

THAT FATEFUL NIGHT

Now divorced, Hunter would arrive at Tracey's home on November 22nd, 2010.

According to Tracey, he then became enraged when Tracey told him that she had spent the night with a new lover.

"He told me that he was gonna kill me," Tracey recalled. Tracey stated that she tried to escape, running into the closet in order to "get away from the kids and to pray." Tracey's eleven-year-old son from a previous relationship was in the home as was the four-year-old daughter they have together.

Hunter caught up with her and knocked her to the ground. He tied a belt around her ankles and then began choking her.

Half-conscious, Tracey alleged to have been raped and sodomized.

The brutal attack would leave Tracey unconscious. She would wake up the next morning on the bathroom floor.

"I called Hunter," Tracey recalled. "I told him that I was bleeding and that I was hurt and that I needed help. And he told me, 'Fuck you. I hope you die."

Tracey wound up in the emergency room after the attack. Hospital records would show that she had a laceration on her head, bruises, and ligature marks on her feet.

Tracey would then be referred to the Turning Point domestic violence center.

Marian Waters would describe Tracey's injuries as among the worst she had ever seen in a twenty-year career.

Waters would testify that Tracey had suffered a horrific assault. She described her mental state as typical of someone who had just been raped; fearful, jumpy, fearing for her life.

Tracey had suffered a hematoma on her side that was the side of a grapefruit. She also claimed to have experienced rectal nerve damage which would require surgery as well as torn vaginal muscles requiring her to have a hysterectomy.

Police were called and Hunter would be arrested for rape, sodomy, kidnapping and domestic violence.

"And at that point, I feared for my life," Tracey recalled. "And I feared for my children's life."

A HIDDEN AGENDA

Hunter would be freed on bail but Tracey got a restraining order against him. She bought a gun and did not go anywhere unarmed.

She took photos of her injuries on the night of the alleged attack and texted them to Loran. Later, they would take more pictures.

Angered, Hunter would stop paying her spousal and child support. Tracey, however, may have had another scenario in mind for obtaining money.

She had forced Hunter to take out a $103,000 life insurance policy around the time their daughter was born.

On May 24, 2012, the day before Tracey shot Hunter, she would place a call to MetLife that was recorded.

"Thank you for calling MetLife, this is Pam. May I please have your name?"

"Tracey Grissom."

Tracey would then explain that she was angry that her husband stopped making payments on his policy. During their divorce proceedings, he had agreed to continue paying the premiums. Tracey stated she was calling to make sure that they had the correct address on file.

"Is there anything else I can do for you today?

"That's gonna be it!" Tracey said, hanging up.

"Well, May 14th was just like any other day," Tracey said, explaining the call to the insurance company. "However, I had moved four different times. Me and my children were running. We were running from Hunter. So I had called the company to let them know that they had my old address and to make an address change."

FALSE RAPE?

Shelly Standridge was hired by Hunter to defend him in the rape case. She would state that Hunter denied raping or even assaulting Tracey that night. Hunter did, however, admit to the fact that he and his wife had consensual sex that night...Rough consensual sex.

"So that night," Standridge said. "Hunter said that she was depressed and claiming she was going to kill herself. She was saying she wanted their relationship to work."

So she undressed in front of him. Her beauty was always impossible for Hunter to resist.

The two had sex despite Hunter having a new girlfriend at home.

Hunter's aunt, Gina, believed that Tracey wanted to kill Hunter before the rape case went to court.

"He had a new girlfriend, he was living with her," Phelps said. "He was moving on with his life. Hunter would claim that Tracey was jealous, obsessive, even stalked them."

"Hunter had moved on," Hunter's aunt said. "There was some court dates coming up that would prove that Hunter was innocent. There were court dates coming up that he would get visitation to his daughter. She had a lot to lose."

Tracey was on the anti-anxiety drug Klonopin. Hunter would tell his attorney that Tracey would take more than her prescribed dose. Because of this, she fell and cut her head. Hunter would then leave the house around 10:30 pm and go to his father's house. Tracey would call him hours later, at 3:20 am.

Hunter would state that Tracey had called to threaten him. She told him if he didn't want the responsibility of the children then she would make it where he would never be able to see them again.

Hunter's attorney did not know what Tracey's motive was for crying rape. She was very upset that he had a girlfriend.

MORE LIES...

Hunter would be arrested nearly twelve hours later, to his total shock.

Tracey would give her side of the story to the police which later is proven to be false.

She would tell police that Hunter had thrown her against the bathtub around 10 pm and claim to be unconscious until 4 am the next morning.

"But her phone records show she was on the phone all night, so she was never unconscious," Standridge said. "She was also using her data at 10:42 that night. She was using it again at 10:50 that night. ... She sends a text to her boyfriend at 1:49 am. She sends a text to her friend at 2:07 am. She sends another text to her boyfriend at 2:07 am."

Tracey would blame the calls on Hunter.

"All I do know is I was not the only person using my phone that night," Tracey said, suggesting that Hunter used her phone.

Medical records would show that Tracey's head wound was "purely superficial".

Only one suture was needed.

Furthermore, there was nothing on the medical record to support the fact that Tracey experienced vaginal and rectal tears. She did have bruises on her ankle and legs but the photos taken by police at the emergency room would not resemble the same photos that Tracey and her friend Loran would take days later. In the photos taken at the emergency room, an area of Tracey's body has no bruises. Days later, there is discoloration.

Tracey's attorney would blame the discrepancy on "blood thinners" which would cause Tracey to bruise easily.

There was also a discrepancy in her phone records. She would take a photo of her inner thigh, a deep bruise. This area of her body was not photographed by police during her emergency room visit. But on December 9th, almost two weeks later, Tracey took a photo of her inner thigh with the deep bruise

"He (Hunter) told me that he would make it to where nobody would ever want me," Tracey said after a 2010 attack. "I didn't report it because I thought he would kill me."

THE FINAL STRAW

Tracey woke up pissed on May 15th, 2012.

Hunter had been ordered to pay $2,100 a month for the rest of his life. He was not complying with the court order claiming that he was "out of work."

Tracey stated that she was on her way to a job interview when she saw a Grissom Construction sign out of the corner of her eye.

She stated that her initial plan was to take a photograph of Hunter at the job site in order to show proof that he was working as part of her litigation.

"I was getting ready to take the picture and when I looked up he was standing almost directly towards the front of the boat trailer," Tracey said. "He was looking back directly at me. He had this face, that's like mean - just, I don't know how to describe it. I mean, I see it over and over like it's right there all the time. He flipped me the bird, which to me was kinda like, 'Yeah I'm workin. Screw you.' And at that point, I panicked. At that point, I didn't know what else to do except to defend myself."

Tracey started firing. The first shot hit Hunter in the arm. He started to run and she fired again repeatedly. One of the bullets punctured Hunter's heart and he died of massive internal bleeding.

William Dockery was working with Hunter and was an eyewitness to the shooting. Hunter had turned to Dockery before the shooting and told him to "call the law". Before Dockery could pick up his cell phone, Tracey had commenced shooting.

Tracey then pulled out her own cell phone and called the cops on herself. She tearfully described that she had just murdered her husband.

CONFESSION

Tracey told detectives exactly what was going through her mind when she came upon Hunter at the construction site.

"Tell me about what happened," the detective said. "What led up to...what's going on."

"In November of 2010, he beat me unconscious and raped me...and, and left me for dead....and, and I finally pressed charges against him and he told me that he would make my life a living hell...and that's what he's done."

"What, what happened this morning that led up to you going..."

"I was going to work and I saw him...and he's been claiming that he-he's not working. And, so I pulled in there to take a picture of him...cause it was the truck that's still in my name...and the boat that's still in my name...and the trailer that's still in my name...He just stared at me and flipped me off...and I just went in there and shot him...I just shot him, I shot him, and I shot him."

Tracey would be distraught and tearful during her interrogation room confession. A few weeks later, however, she would call the insurance company to let them know that Hunter had died.

"Well, I was actually calling because I didn't know what I needed to do ... Hunter passed away May 15th and I actually am going a court case right now because it was due to self-defense..."

Hunter's family went ballistic over this. Tracey would claim that she had no money but she continued to pay his life insurance premiums.

"Even through the times when she's screamin' that she's destitute and has no money ... she continued to pay life insurance premium," Hunter's mother said.

"I don't think my sister concocted a story," Tracey's sister said. "Just so she could get insurance money. ... But that's all they (the prosecution) had."

THE TRIAL

Tracey's allegations of rape and sodomy would not be allowed in court testimony. She was allowed, however, to detail the effects of Hunter's abuse on her were.

Taking the stand, Tracey would lift up her shirt in court and show herself wearing a colostomy bag. She stated that she had undergone several surgeries after her husband's daily rapes wherein she suffered permanent rectal and vaginal damage.

Hunter's family was then allowed to speak at the hearing.

"This tremendous loss has changed me," Hunter's mother, Melanie Garner said. "And I don't know how to change back."

Chloe, Hunter's sister, had a victim's services officer read her letter in court.

"Tracey is psychotic," Chloe wrote. "She is the most selfish person human being on this earth."

"Every mother should pray every night that your son doesn't fall in love with someone like Tracey," Hunter's aunt, Gina Grissom said. "There have been lots of allegations against Hunter. We've never believed anything that has come out of her (Tracey's) mouth."

His aunt then looked directly at Tracey.

"Hunter was proud of his name. Why would you still choose to use our name, and bring it down?" suggesting that if Tracey hated him so much why didn't she go revert to her maiden name after the divorce.

The jurors would find Tracey guilty of murder. She would be sentenced to twenty-five years in prison.

One of the jurors, Janice Kelly, would contact Grissom's attorney Warren Freeman the morning after the trial. She had remorse over her decision and said that she wouldn't have convicted her had they had the rapes and abuse allegations been introduced as evidence.

"I feel I made a mistake," Kelly said. "If I had to do it over again, we'd have had a hung jury. We didn't get her side. She did not get a fair trial."

"We voted to convict because there was no dispute that Tracey shot Hunter," the jury foreman wrote in a letter that was addressed in the courthouse. "Jurors didn't believe prosecutor claims that she did it in order to collect a life insurance policy. We felt the shooting was a crime of passion, not for financial gain and that she should be sentenced accordingly. I wish we had seen evidence of the rape allegation. We feel that she just 'lost it.'"

"It's not fair, it's not fair!" Tracey sobbed as she was led out of the courthouse and to jail.

"We think the sentencing was too harsh," Tracey's attorney Warren Freeman said. "Considering you have the foreperson of the jury actually saying, we don't feel like she should be punished according to being found guilty of murder. Let's just say that there will be a basis for a new trial, and part of it will be something that the jurors saw that they weren't supposed to see and I'm going to just leave it at that until I file my motion."

"My son died running for his life," Hunter's mother said. "I don't know what was running through his mind but I hear him say 'momma.'"

"People who think that I murdered him in cold blood," Tracey said. "Either don't know the whole story or don't know everything that's happened.

Tracey was asked on CBS' 48 hours if she regretted pulling the trigger on that fateful day.

"No," she said flatly. "Because if I hadn't I would be dead. I truly believe that."

"She has a way of making everything she does look right," Hunter's aunt, Gina scoffed.

KILLER CON WOMAN : THE TRUE STORY OF DEE DEE MOORE

SUSAN GRAHAM

Abraham Shakespeare didn't have too much going on in life. He was the son of an orange picker limited to menial day jobs. He never held a job where he made more than eight dollars an hour.

He didn't have a car, a driver's license or a credit card. He dropped out of school and could barely read or write.

The lanky 6'5" inch, 190 lbs laborer would patrol around town, looking for something to steal or people to assault.

He would go to jail two times and when he was released in 1995, he went to live with his mother.

Trying to cobble together any kind of life, Abraham would find work as a garbage man. Then he worked in a restaurant washing dishes before gaining employment on a shipping and receiving dock.

He was on the road to nowhere unless he hit the lottery.

On November 15th, 2006, however, he did just that. He rode shotgun with a truck driver named Michael Ford. They were making meat deliveries to restaurants in the area.

Ford then stopped off at the Town Star mini-mart in Frostproof. Abraham stayed in the car and Ford asked if he wanted anything.

Abraham only had ten dollars in his pocket. He asked for two quick picks in the lotto drawing.

Ford would buy the winning ticket for Abraham. The numbers 6, 12, 13, 34, 42, and 52 netted Abraham the $30 million dollar jackpot.

Ford would then sue him for what he believed should be "his share of the proceeds". He wanted no less than $1 million dollars and later claimed that Abraham had stolen the two tickets from his wallet.

"He knows the truth," Abraham said of Ford. "I know the truth."

The lawsuit hit the news wires but it took the jury only an hour to rule that Abraham did not steal the winning ticket from Ford's wallet.

"From my background investigation, he (Abraham) was always kind of a transient type," Ford's attorney, Michael Laurato, said. "If it wasn't for his criminal record, he kind of didn't exist."

Abraham would elect to take the lump sum cash payment of $17 million instead of the thirty annual payments totaling $30 million.

LET THE PARTY BEGIN

"Abraham was suddenly given the keys to the good life," Miami journalist Zack Jacobs said. "He threw a big party and suddenly found himself surrounded by numerous hangers-on. They partied and wined and dined. He paid them back for their attention with lavish gifts and cash prizes."

The first thing Abraham did was pay off his back child support which totaled almost $9,000. He then placed $1 million dollars into a trust fund for his son. He then gave his stepfather $1 million dollars and his three step-sisters $250,000 apiece. But his generosity didn't stop with his family. He paid off a $185,000 mortgage for a friend, $60,000 for another friend and another $53,000 for a mortgage for a man he had been "knowing for years."

Word of Abraham's open wallet began to spread.

His brother's best friend came over and he gave him $40,000. He gave his mother $12,000 and his sister $10,000.

In other words, he became the family ATM.

"Abraham's mother was the only one who grew wary of all of the well-wishers," Jacobs said. "She worked in a cafeteria at the local junior college and was a church-going woman. She thought that money was evil and was leery of Abraham getting so much of it. She knew that the folks coming around were just doing it out of their own selfish desires. They all wanted something from Abraham whereas before they wouldn't even give him the time of day."

Abraham would not heed his mother's warnings. He would write checks to whoever tugged at his heart strings. This meant paying for funerals of loved ones and people he didn't know.

"Abraham really had no idea of the value of money," Jacobs said. "And that isn't an insult. Remember, here was a guy who was in and out of jail. He never made more than eight dollars an hour. So, in his mind, seventeen million dollars would last forever. So, I think like most lottery winners, the initial euphoria simply consumed him. He was not thinking annuities and investments. He was simply enjoying all the indulgences and attention money could buy."

Abraham had other ideas about money.

"The Bible states it's better to give than to receive," Abraham said, explaining his gift giving.

Arnold Levine, another attorney who represented Ford in the suit, described Abraham as an "angry guy" whose made sure that his gifts came with "strings attached."

"My sense," Levine said, "was that some of his family members were unhappy with the amount of money he had parceled out to them. Were there people who were jealous? I would assume so."

After he gifted his relatives, Abraham began indulging himself. He purchased a Nissan Altima and a Rolex watch from a pawnshop. He then bought a 2006 F-150 pickup, a 2007 BMW 750i and finally a $1.1 million dollar home.

The brick and stucco home came replete with security cameras and a gate. It was over 6,500 square feet with an enclosed pool and a two two-car garages.

Aside from these extravagances, Abraham regretted winning the lottery. He was subject to constant requests for money from friends and even people he didn't know.

"I'd have been better off broke," Abraham later said to his brother. He then confided to another friend that "I thought all these people were my friends, but then I realized all they want is just money."

But Abraham only saw the tip of the iceberg. He was about to meet someone who didn't just want a little of his money. She wanted all of it.

And she was willing to kill him to get it.

Her name was Dorice Donegan Moore, better known as "Dee Dee".

ENTER THE CON

Dee Dee was a self-styled entrepreneur. A tall and shapely blonde, she was thirty-five years old and had a twenty-six-year-old boyfriend.

"Dee Dee was the kind of psychopath that could focus on her mark and not take no for an answer," Jacobs said. "She had an over the top, type-A personality. She could make her mark feel as if they were the only person in the world that mattered. She could look you straight in the eye and lie without any compunction."

She read about Abraham's story in the paper and the wheels in her head began to turn.

Dee Dee Morgan had tried to meet Abraham through his friends and even called his mother to no avail. Finally, she found out who sold him the million dollar estate, a realtor named Barbara Jackson.

"When I met her (Dee Dee), she was in a wheelchair," Jackson said. "She said she was in a car accident."

Dee Dee listened as Jackson told others about Abraham and how he changed their outlook about money. He insisted that it wasn't about money at all. It was about helping people. Jackson encouraged others to embrace this similar outlook.

Dee Dee feigned interest as she introduced herself to Jackson, telling the realtor that she was a writer. She said that she wanted to write an article or maybe even a book about Abraham, documenting his life so far and his viewpoints about money.

Jackson acquiesced and arranged for Dee Dee to meet Abraham.

"When she came to the house," Jackson said, "She jumped out of a Hummer, walking. And she was on heels. She said she healed herself through scuba therapy. It wasn't even two weeks."

Both Jackson and Abraham listened to Dee Dee's spiel. She spoke of her admiration for Abraham's philanthropy and wanted the world to hear about it.

Abraham was naïve and fell for the con. He agreed to have Dee Dee do the story about him.

"Abraham was vulnerable to someone with the manipulative charm of Dee Dee," Jacobs said. "Here was a guy who was about as down on his luck as you can get. Then he is a multi-millionaire overnight. He gets all the attention and love that was denied him his whole life. He really didn't know who to trust. Then along comes Dee Dee. She's well-spoken, well-dressed and seems to know what's going on inside his head."

What neither Abraham or Jackson didn't know was that Dee Dee Moore had a history of con artistry.

She had once staged a hoax that she believed would enable her to keep a Lincoln Navigator which was about to be repossessed. She had fallen hopelessly behind on the payments and had someone put the car in a garage. She then pretended that she was carjacked, kidnapped and raped by "three Mexican guys."

Dee Dee went all out in the pre-meditated scheme. She taped her wrists and threw herself out of someone else's moving car to make her injuries look real.

"This was an elaborate ruse," Jacobs said. "She had a friend drive her down the highway and she propelled herself out of the vehicle. She then tore apart her own clothes, smeared her make-up and started to cry. All of this was done as she crawled down the side of the highway, waiting for a sympathetic motorist to come pick her up."

A Good Samaritan would come along and take her to the hospital. She detailed her story to the police and medical staff, even going so far as to take a rape exam.

But her scheme was exposed and she would plead no contest to the charge and get probation. Always on the make for a new mark, Dee Dee needed another scheme. When she read about the lottery winning Abraham and his lawsuit with Ford, she had found herself a new patsy.

"Dee Dee couldn't make it on the straight road," Jacobs said. "Her businesses, whatever she was doing, were not generating any sufficient revenue for her to maintain the lifestyle that she felt she was entitled to. So she had to swindle and con. Unfortunately for Abraham, he got in her crosshairs."

LET'S START A BUSINESS

"Dee Dee was a master manipulator," Jacobs said. "She befriended Abraham first and gained his trust. She picked up on the fact that he had all of these people after his money. So she did some reverse psychology on him. She convinced Abraham that she was the opposite, that she would never take anything from him."

Convinced of Dee Dee's trustworthiness, Abraham agreed to start an LLC with the woman. They titled the business "Abraham Shakespeare LLC".

"He agreed to do this under the provision that anyone who asked for money would have to go through her," Jacobs said. "She convinced him that she had his best interests in mind. But in her mind, she saw him as a dupe. A rube. She was telling herself 'I'm going to work this guy. I'm going to work this guy and take everything he has. Schmuck!'"

The corporation was in Abraham's name but the funds were under the control of Dee Dee.

Once she had control of the LLC, Dee Dee proceeded to withdraw $1 million dollars.

"She had totally hoodwinked poor Abraham," Jacobs said. "Now everything was under her own company banner, some type of bullshit medical company. Nothing came out of Abraham's account without her signature."

Abraham had stopped giving money to people without recompense. He then became the town ATM around his native Plant City. Judy Haggins helped him keep track of the loans as to who owed what.

Judy knew Abraham for fifteen years and she was taken aback that Dee Dee was involving herself in Abraham's affairs.

"When Abraham got ready to go to the bank one day to see about his money, (Moore) immediately called me on the phone," Judy said in the recording of her conversation with Smith. "You've got to stall him, Judy. He can't go to the bank."

Judy then received money from Abraham's account to pay for her help. "It was a little bit of money for me. (Moore) felt like Abraham should pay me to take his mama. Abraham used to come to me and say, 'Now you know that white woman got my money, she can do anything to me.' I said, 'Abraham, you can go get your money.'"

Judy could not stall Abraham, however. He drove over to Dee Dee's home to confront her. He wanted his money back under his name. All of it.

"It isn't working out," Abraham said. "I am going to the bank and straighten this shit out."

Dee Dee did her best to try and talk him out of it but Abraham was resolute in his decision.

"This was her worst fear come to light," Jacobs said. "Her mark had figured her out. Abraham was being nice about it but if he went to the bank there would be a huge investigation. She would go to jail. She couldn't let that happen."

Dee Dee would play along and told Abraham that she had all of his money in a safe she had behind her desk. She walked over to the safe and opened it.

But none of Abraham's money inside.

The only thing she had inside was a gun.

Spinning around, she pointed the pistol at Abraham.

"Aw shit," Abraham said. "Don't do it."

Dee Dee didn't listen. She fired twice, hitting Abraham in his chest, killing him. She then rolled up his body in a tarp and stole his cell phone.

"Her idea was to tap into people who owed Abraham money," Jacobs said. "She scanned through all of Abraham's text messages and realized how many people owed him money. Close to three million dollars. She figured she could impersonate him via cell phone messages and collect on these debts. An insane plan to any rational human being. But to do Dee Dee, a psychopath who thought she was smarter than everyone, it looked like easy money."

CLEANING UP THE MESS

Dee Dee contacted her ex-husband, James Moore to do some "yard work". She asked if he could dig a hole in her yard in April of 2009.

James could only scratch his head at the odd request.

"Why?" James asked.

"Oh, I just need a hole to bury some concrete and trash in," Dee Dee said. "I don't want my landlord to see all the stuff out here."

James would dig the hole then leave. But Dee Dee would call him back two hours later, however, asking him to fill the hole.

James, who was paid to do yard work by Dee Dee, agreed to fill the hole but didn't see what she had placed inside as it was now dark.

Dee Dee had placed Abraham's body in the hole.

A BLOOD TRAIL

Dee Dee continued to cover her tracks. She stole Abraham's cell phone and sent text messages to his family and friends, pretending to be the man she had just killed.

"Have to get away for awhile," Dee Dee texted Abraham's mother under his own cell phone number. "Going to the Caribbean."

The people receiving the texts became suspicious, however, because the texts didn't sound like him. Abraham was functionally illiterate. They would then text back for clarification and would be ignored. His mother grew especially worried. She texted back and told Abraham to call her.

His family now stalled, Dee Dee turned her attention to Abraham's assets. She used her own company, American Medical Professionals, to purchase Abraham's home.

In February of 2009, Dee Dee would purchase a 2008 Corvette for her boyfriend for $70,000. She would pay for this vehicle with a cashier's check from her American Medical Professionals, LLC business account.

"She had a boy toy," Jacobs said. "And she lavished the kid with money that she stole from Abraham. This included a house and a Corvette."

The following month, she purchased a 2009 Hummer for herself for $90,000 before taking her boy toy on a luxury vacation.

Abraham's family would report him missing on November 9th of 2009, almost seven months after his presumed date of death.

"Abraham told a friend that he was tired," Jacobs said. "He was tired of people constantly pressing him for money. So he hinted to more than one friend that he was 'fittin' to get outta here.' When no one saw him for a long period of time, they just wrote it off to the fact that he had gotten fed up with the situation and left town. It was only after they had not seen him for such a prolonged period of time that they finally reported it."

When questioned by police, Dee stated that Abraham left town. She said he was either in Texas, Jamaica, Puerto Rico, Florida or was admitted into a hospital.

"He was sick of people asking him for money," Dee Dee said. "I helped him leave town. He didn't tell me where he was going."

Dee Dee would state that the reason Abraham was taken off the account was because he didn't want to pay taxes. She couldn't give a reason for the fact that over $1 million was withdrawn only days after his name was taken off the LLC listing. She then said that Abraham also didn't want to pay child support.

Thinking she needed more accomplices, Dee Dee thought she could buy some. She approached the mother of one of Abraham's sons, telling her that she would give her a $200,000 house if she would lie to detectives and tell them that she had seen Abraham in recent days. She then paid a cousin of Abraham, Cedric Edom, over $5,000 to send his mother a birthday card and imply that it was from Abraham.

Abraham had not contacted his family since April of 2009. They believed that he was off on a Caribbean island somewhere enjoying his money.

"On a cruise," Dee Dee texted through Abraham's cell phone. "Having a great time."

But Abraham was far from the Jamaican isles. He was buried in five feet of dirt under a concrete slab.

LEAVING FINGERPRINTS BEHIND

Dee Dee sold her Hummer to a friend of a Chevrolet dealer for only $49,000. She said that she needed to get quick cash. Three weeks later, she had lunch with Elizabeth Walker, Abraham's mother.

Dee Dee also typed up a letter which she wanted to pass off as coming from Abraham.

"She had a brand-new laptop, set up and a printer, (and) she had a rubber-type gloves on," Abraham's friend, Gregory Smith recalled. "And a scarf pullover-type thing over her head."

'Don't worry about Dee,' the letter read. 'There are too many people that know I left. I gave her enough money... she would not take anything from me unless I agreed.'

She then had Gregory call Abraham's mother and pretend he was Abraham.

"Hi Mom," Gregory said. "I'm fine. Had to get away."

"Who is this?" Elizabeth said. "You're not Abe! Who are you?"

Dee Dee made her first strategic error here. Elizabeth Walker knew her son's voice and the voice on the other end did not belong to him. She contacted police who investigated and eventually caught up with Gregory Smith.

Gregory would cooperate and play informant against Dee Dee. This would involve the use of an undercover police officer to aid Gregory.

Dee Dee had told Gregory that she needed someone to take the fall for Abraham's murder. She told Gregory to find someone that would accept $50,000 in exchange for declaring themselves guilty of Abraham's murder. Gregory told the investigators of the scheme and they had an undercover cop, Mike Smith, come along with Gregory as they arranged a deal.

"I did it (help the undercover operation) because when they explained to me what was going on and they said they had their suspicions that something like I told them," Gregory Smith said. "He had money. He could have went anywhere. Anybody was saying anything. I didn't know where he was, really didn't go into where he was. But the deal is when they came to me and they explained to me that there was an investigation going on. And I wouldn't get in no trouble and I could walk out of there right now, but they needed some help to find Abraham. I said I'd see what I could do. "

Dee Dee met with the undercover officer. The con artist was about to be conned.

"The undercover officer explained himself as someone up on federal charges," Jacobs said. "He was about to be sent to jail for life. He could take the $50,000 and live it up in his final days. But what he needed from Dee Dee was proof that he was the killer."

Dee Dee took the bait. She showed the undercover detective where she had buried Abraham, five feet under a concrete slab in her backyard.

"I need you to dig him up," Dee Dee said. "And then burn his body."

She also gave the undercover cop the gun that was used to kill Abraham.

"She gave Mike the map of her backyard," Jacobs said. "She was so blinded by her own need to get away with the crime that she didn't she that she was being played. He was wired up the whole time. They had everything they needed on tape. She confessed to everything."

"Don't forget to bring the marshmallows," Dee Dee said to the undercover cop when she told him to burn Abraham's body.

EXCAVATING THE BODY

Digging at the site, the police unearthed Abraham's body. They then brought Dee Dee back in for another interrogation.

The con woman would give them multiple stories. First, she said that drug dealers killed Abraham. Then it was his attorney that had him killed. Then she would blame her fourteen-year-old son before finally saying that she killed Abraham herself...but only in self-defense.

Dee Dee's manipulations didn't stop there.

She told one of the investigating detectives, David Clark, that she hoped they could eventually have sex once the investigation was over.

"I find you very attractive," Dee Dee said to Clark.

Detectives would estimate that Abraham died around April 6th or 7th. They would take Dee Dee into custody and charge her with accessory to murder.

"The money was like a curse to him," Dee Dee said to reporters. "And now it's become a curse to me. God knows I would never take another human being's life."

COURTROOM DRAMA

During the trial, Dee Dee began making threats to jurors. Two of the jurors would state that Gregory Smith had intimidated them in the parking lot. Smith, a convicted felon five times over, denied the charges. The judge would ask one of the jurors if she had felt threatened by Dee Dee or any members of her family or friends and the juror simply responded that she wanted to feel safe.

The judge would then caution Dee Dee from making 'facial expressions' at the jurors as she would stare stone-faced at some of them, trying to intimidate.

The jury would deliberate for three hours before finding Moore guilty of the first-degree murder charge.

"She got every bit of his money," Assistant State Attorney Jay Pruner said. "He found out about it and threatened to kill her. She killed him first."

Dee Dee's attorney Byron Hileman argued otherwise, stating that there were other suspects that the prosecution should have went after.

"There were a lot of people who owed Mr. Shakespeare a lot of money," Hileman said. "One guy owed him a million dollars. The police focused on Dee Dee Moore and they didn't even consider other people."

Judge Emmett Battles called Dee Dee "the most manipulative person I have ever seen" and that she was "cold, calculating and cruel."

Dee Dee Moore would be convicted of first-degree murder on December 20th, 2012.

She would be sentenced to life in prison without the possibility of parole with an additional 25 years.

"'I'm missing my little brother," Abraham's brother Robert Brown said after the proceedings. "What ain't gonna be back no more. Dead and gone, and everything. He ain't coming back."

Dee Dee maintains that she is innocent and that her trial did not have evidence that would have exonerated her. She states that she is writing two books as well as penning poetry.

"Friends are a gift,
You give yourself.
When life has too many,
Mountains to climb alone." - Dee Dee Moore

KIM SNIBSON

CURLY SIMON

87

"Why is this happening?"

Those may have been Greg Hosa's last audible words as Andrew Flentjar and Stacy Lea-Caton brutally forced him to the ground. The answer Flentjar gave would shock not just Hosa, but both of his attackers. For it was that response that would have allowed both Flentjar and Lea-Caton to realize that they were not part of the just cause they had believed themselves to be, but were in fact at the mercy of Kim Snibson's deluded and volatile plan.

Kim Snibson is a master manipulator who was envious of the life Greg Hosa and his wife Kathryn McKay had built together. Most notably, their horse farm. Situated in Nowra, New South Wales, Champagne Shires would be considered a small property when compared to the amount of land horse farms usually covered. Still, despite its modest size, it was far grander that Snibson could ever hope to own herself. For her, Champagne Shires was the perfect combination of all her fondest desires and life passions. Living next door to her dream made reality, it didn't take long for her fantasies of owning the property to become a perceived right. Snibson's greed led her to believe that she deserved Champagne Shires, while her ego convinced her that she could have it, if only the current owners were dealt away with.

Once Hosa and McKay had agreed to stable her horse, Snibson had the perfect excuse to visit her neighbors. She would come by often and grew to know both Hosa and McKay well. This access only fuelled her lust for the property and her disdain for the happy owners. Unaware of Snibson's feelings towards them, Hosa and McKay remained kind and generous to their neighbor. On one known occasion, Snibson had fallen behind in payments and owed the couple $300 for the care of her horse. Hosa and McKay had agreed to continue to stable her horse and told Snibson that she could pay them when she was able. This generosity did not provoke gratitude in Snibson, but instead fed into her increasing resentment. By this time she had begun to believe that she could force the couple to sign over the rights to Champagne Shires to her, kill them, and live happily on the property without consequence. Rationally this plan is ludicrous, but given her past success, Snibson believed it to be perfect.

Years earlier Snibson had inherited her house in Calymea Street, Nowra Hill, from an elderly woman named Judith Plankas. It was this property that had made her a neighbor of Hosa and McKay, and ultimately, it was in this house that the couple would be murdered. But it wasn't until after her arrest that questions began to arise as to exactly why and how Ms Plankas came to deed the property to Snibson.

In an interview with Take-5 Magazine, Snibson's ex-husband recalled how Ms Snibson had befriended Ms Plankas. At the time, the elderly dog breeder had been diagnosed with cancer and had needed help taking care of her animals. Snibson had been quick to offer assistance and for a while must have struck the sickly Ms Plankas as a Godsend. But, as Mr Snibson told Take-5 Magazine, "Kim got hold of powerful tranquilizers and quietly killed the older dogs." Perhaps accustomed to Kim's crueler actions, or blinded by devotion, it is believed that Mr Snibson neglected to inform Plankas of what Kim had done. By all appearances, Ms Plankas had no idea what kind of woman she had welcomed into her home.

"Then on April 17, 2003," Mr Snibson recalled, "Judith's condition suddenly worsened. She changed her will that night, leaving the house to Kim, and died the next day."

This would not be the first time Mr Snibson had been privy to the threat Kim posed to those around her. And it would not be the only time his failure to believe or act lead to disastrous consequences. In the same interview, he revealed a conversation he had once had with a woman named Rebecca. She had only been 15-years-old when Ms Snibson had convinced her to move out of the home and in with the Snibson family.

"We've got a free babysitter," Ms Snibson had announced when she had brought the teenager home, according to her ex-husband. He went on to say that, "later, Rebecca sought me out and what she had to say rocked me. Kim had kept a horse at a stable owned by an elderly couple and Rebecca said (that Kim) talked about tying them up, making them sign over their property to her and killing them."

Still, it would seem that Mr Snibson was not then willing to believe his wife capable of such things. But Rebecca wasn't Snibson's first nor only attempt at recruiting accomplices in her murder plot. Nor was the teenager's confession the only one to be dismissed. Armed with vicious lies and a willingness to manipulate all those around her, Snibson approached numerous people. Perhaps it is a testament to her skill at manipulation, or her ability to choose those reluctant to cause a stir without any solid evidence, but many of the people she approached never spoke of the conversations until after she had been arrested. Mr Snibson claimed that was when he began to receive calls from dozens of friends, most of which started with 'I've been wanting to tell you this for years'.

"Then they'd tell me about an affair she'd had or how she'd tried to enlist them in a desperate scheme to have someone beaten up or killed," he told Take-5 Magazine. He also spoke about how a friend had told him that 'Kim had wanted an old lady beaten up because she said her son had molested one of your girls'. "Nobody has touched my daughters," Mr Snibson said. "It was a fantasy made up by Kim to get others to do terrible things for her."

With so many people aware of the true, malicious nature of Snibson, it is baffling how few people voiced their concerns to law enforcement. Snibson continued her search for willing participants until she found two men who believed her lies. Her first recruit was Andrew Flentjar. He was a neighbor of the Snibson family, although Mr Snibson insists that he didn't know Flentjar that well, and had believed that Snibson hadn't either.

"She didn't socialize with (him) or stay for a cuppa," he had said in an interview. But still Snibson had managed to make the otherwise reasonable man willing to help her in her plan to kidnap and assault Mr Hosa.

"Andrew was told by Kim that the couple had sexually abused her child and had videoed the episode," Paul Leask, a Crown Prosecutor for New South Wales, reviled on the television show Deadly Women.

In her interview on the same television show, a journalist for Illawarra Mercury Newspaper, Veronica Apap, attested that there had been "no evidence at any time in court that Kathryn or Greg had engaged in anything like that." Still, Flintjar believed the story Snibson wove and, under the impression that her plan only involved minor assault as justice for her daughter, agreed to help.

Snibson then approached Stacy Lea-Caton, a former neighbor who had been in trouble with the law. Mr Snibson remembers Lea-Caton as being a man who continuously worked to create a notable reputation for himself as a dangerous man.

"You would be talking about normal things," Mr Snibson told Ms Apap during an interview, "and Stacey would come in with something bigger or better. He talked about his criminal history, stuff like that."

Mr Snibson went on to say that when it came to Mr Lea-Caton he "didn't believe anything he told me", and that, "I didn't think he would go very well in a fight, myself. He is not this tough person he was making himself out to be."

Ms Snibson, however, saw a potential for violence in Lea-Caton and knew just how to bring it to the surface.

During a visit she tested the waters by telling him a lie similar to the one she had recruited Flintjar with. According to Leask, "Stacey Lea-Caton was told by her that the couple had drugged her, sexually assaulted her, and videoed the episode."

Once again there she could produce any evidence in support of her claims, nor could later investigators. According to Apap, "It seems to be a total fantasy on her part" and Mr Snibson has stated that "Greg Hosa was a thoroughly decent person who did not deserve such terrible lies to be made up about him, let alone die so needlessly." Still, Snibson was convincing enough to for Lea-Coton to push aside his desire to get his life back on track and he soon found himself alongside Flintjar, embroiled in Snibson's supposed plan for vigilante justice.

"She employed a means of modulating the story depending on the person who was the recipient of it. To press the right buttons." Leask asserted. "The theme was always one of sexual impropriety and of course, nothing excites people's sympathy more than that."

With her two accomplices waiting for instructions, Snibson put her plan into action on January 28th, 2006. It was easy to lure Hosa to her home. The 56-year-old man didn't suspect that anything might be wrong when Snibson called and asked him to come over.

"He came quickly after that conversation occurred," Apap said in her Deadly Women interview. "He didn't think that he was in any danger or that there would be any problem."

Lea-Carton and Flintjar swarmed Hosa as he entered the Snibson home. Using a slab of wood they struck him on the head and forced him to the ground. The men then proceeded to hogtie Hosa, forcing him onto his stomach and binding his legs to his hands. It was during this attack that Hosa asked his assailants "why is this happening?" While the exact wording cannot be determined, it is reported that Flintjar responded by accusing Hosa of pedophilia.

With this declaration both of Snibson's henchmen realized that they had been lied to. They were blindsided by the revelation yet, having participated in assault and kidnapping, and still unaware of just how malicious Snibson's intentions were, neither felt they were in a position to leave. Snibson deceit had taken them past the point of no return and both were at a loss at what to do next. This afforded Snibson the perfect environment to maintain control.

While the men watched over a struggling Hosa, Snibson called his wife and 'confessed' that she and Hosa had been having an affair. It was a story that few would believe and later would be seen by their family as adding a foul insult to considerable injury. Jan Keily, a sister of McKay, would attest that they family was 'disgusted' by the claim. But on that night, it was enough to draw McKay into Snibon's trap.

Just like her husband, 44-year-old McKay was set upon by Lea-Carton and Flintjar. She too was hogtied and gagged by having a sock forced into her mouth and taped into place. Once again the men found themselves forced into a situation far from what they had been expecting when Snibson left to retrieve two 44-gallon drums from Champagne Shires and brought them to the house.

After shoving Ms McKay into one of the drums Snibson disclosed the needlessly cruel method she had chosen in order to kill McKay. "She murdered Kathryn by wrapping tape around her face and eyes and nose," Leask described.

Many factors must be considered when determining how long it would take an individual to suffocate to death. First, oxygen deprivation renders the victim unconscious. If they are still unable to breath brain damage will begin. As a general guide, it is believed to take approximately 5-6 minutes for death to occur. Snibson, Lea-Carton, and Flintjar stood by and watched McKay struggle for this entire length of time. When arrested, all three would give varying statements as to what exactly had happened that night, but in all versions, the two men who had not agreed to murder still made no attempt to save Ms McKay.

When Snibson turned her attention back to Hosa, she had a different method in mind for his execution. According to Leask, "Kim killed Greg Hosa by garrotting him with electrical wire. Kim killed them both deliberately and methodically." And once again, her now reluctant accomplices failed to put an end to her actions.

As night fell the trio loaded the two barrels, each now filled with the corpses of a once loving couple, into the back of Snibson's truck. Together the three drove to a remote patch of the Tomerong State Forest. Here she doused the remains of Ms McKay and Mr Hosa with petrol and set them alight.

As Leask stated, "Incinerating the bodies was done for no other purpose than to destroy evidence that those two poor people had ever been to Kim's house that day."

For all her obsession and manipulation, it took only hours for Snibson's plan to come undone. As it would turn out, Mr Snibson's reading of Stacey Lea-Caton's character had been far more reliable that Kim's had been. The only known criminal within the trio, Lea-Carton was unable to suppress his guilty conscious and within hours of leaving Snibson confessed to his sister and her husband. The series of events he told them had been highly edited but it was still damning enough that the young couple had insisted that he tell the authorities. At 2:30am they had taken him to the Nowra Police Station to report the crime. According to police, Lea-Caton had originally stated that he had seen a man and woman tried up at the farm and was worried that they might come to harm. By 8:00am they had arrested Snibson. A whole day hadn't passed by the time police located the remains of Greg Hosa and Kathryn McKay. Superintendent Kyle Stewart would describe the discovery as a "horrific scene", while Leask provided greater detail. "All that remained of Kathryn was her right foot and little remained of Greg."

But even when caught Snibson was far from willing to admit to her actions. In her statements to the police, she was a hapless witness to a domestic disturbance that spiraled out of control. According to Snibson, she had informed Ms McKay that she had been having an affair with Mr Hosa. Hosa had come to her home first, followed by and enraged Ms McKay. Once there, the couple had begun to argue. The confrontation soon grew volatile and in the heat of the moment Lea-Caton had picked up a bird perch and struck Mr Hose over the head hard enough that he fell to the ground. She recounted how this hadn't deterred Ms McKay who had then turned her anger onto Snibson herself. McKay had become so furious that she had 'come at' Snibson. This had forced Flentjar, who had also happened to be present, to tackle the older woman to keep her from harming Snibson.

"She fell back and hit her head on the pantry and fell on the floor," Snibson told police. She further went on to explain that is was after Ms McKay had been injured that Lea-Caton's murderous intent rose to the surface. In Snibson's version of events, it was Lea-Caton that strangled Hosa with a rope before forcing her to wrap tape around McKay's head until, as she insisted he had instructed, 'she turned blue'. In his final act of depravity, Lea-Caton had been the one to light the bodies on fire.

Her behavior at the trials of her accomplices was a far cry from what others had observed during her own trial. While giving evidence in the New South Wales Supreme Court, Snibson broke down into tears as she described the "gurgling sounds" Mr Hosa made as the life was choked out of him. Snibson would tell the court that she felt "sick to my stomach" about the murders. She continued to say that she thought about it "every single day." She had become so unsettled that Justice Terence Buddin had to adjourn the sentencing hearing for five minutes to give her time to compose herself.

Compared to her behavior and demeanor at other times it was almost possible to believe Ms Snibson was two entirely different people. For Leask, there was no doubt which persona was ligament and which she put on for self-preservation.

"There will be no remorse from Kim Snibson. It's not in her nature," he had said in an interview. He also claimed that Snibson is a person "that lacks the quality that makes us human beings." But perhaps his opinion on Snibson was most elegantly and directly described within his statement, "I have been involved in some shocking crimes involving some dreadful brutality. This case stands out because, in my career, I can only reasonably expect to come across one or two sociopaths. And that's what Kim Snibson is."

It is a sentiment echoed by Candice DeLong, a former criminal profiler for the Federal Bureau of Investigation who often lends her insights to programs such as Deadly Women. "It's unlikely Kim feels remorse for what she did. Sociopaths never do," she said during an interview. She further asserted that "if she ever does emerge from prison, watch out."

It is DeLong's opinion that "Kim is a natural born killer. She wanted to commit murder," but for those like her ex-husband, Snibson is not so clearly an evil woman. While he called her 'pure evil' in an interview with Take-5 Magazine it was also discovered that he had withheld information from investigators in a bid to protect her from prosecution.

"I did tell the truth in all statements," he told the New South Wales Supreme Court. "I left out those couple of sentences from Kim because it sounded very damning to me. I didn't want to see anything bad happen to her. I still had loyalty to Kim even though we had long broken up."

Some of these omitted sentences referred to statements Ms Snibson had made the day after her arrest. According to Mr Snibson, she had said "Don't worry about me, I'm a bad person", and had alluded that she would be 'going away' for 30 years. He further stated that Snibson had said that while she did want to tell him what had happened on the night of the murders her lawyer had instructed her not to talk about it. "She said when she gets to court and has her say, the truth will come out."

Whether Mr Snibson truly believes in his ex-wife's innocence or not, he unwittingly brought more evidence against her. When Detective Sergeant Jason Hogan had asked Mr Snibson to take them to where he as Ms Snibson used to train their dogs for dog sled competitions he had agreed. The location he had led them to had been the where the smoldering barrels holding the remains of McKay and Hosa had been found. In the same day, he had also unknowingly brought the police to the part of Braidwood Road where Mr Hosa's burnt out four-wheel drive had been discovered.

Andrew Wayne Flentjar was the first to be sentenced. He is currently serving a minimum of 10-years for his role in assisting in the kidnapping of Hosa and McKay. Stacey Lea-Caton pleaded guilty to aiding and abetting murder and received a sentence of a minimum 16 years, with the maximum time served of 22-years.

Lea-Caton testified against Snibson during her trail and put a great amount of pressure on her supposed version of events. Combined with the sight of the 44-gallon drums, similar to those used to dispose of McKay and Hosa's remains, which were brought into the courtroom, the cracks in Snibson's account of that night were beginning to show. Whatever the 10 men and 2 women of the jury had truly believed was rendered moot when, approximately halfway through her trial, Snibson changed her plea to guilty.

On September 5th, 2008 Snibson faced her sentencing hearing. By Australian law, those affected by a crime have the right to lodge and read out a victim impact statement to the court and the perpetrator. The friends and family of Hosa and McKay took advantage of this opportunity. Marion, Katheryn McKay's sister, described how the murders had rendered her family into a state similar to 'animals caught in headlights'. In her statement, she explained how she struggled "to find the words for the numbness and traumatic feelings the murders caused the family."

Marion described the impact of their loss and Snibson's actions as being felt "physically, socially, emotionally and psychologically." How her family is no longer able to watch programs about horses or the news, as they stir up too many painful memories. How her work as a counselor has suffered and that the majority of her grief-stricken family has since abandoned their homes in Nowra.

She described McKay and Hosa as loving, community-minded people, and reminded the court and Snibson that her sister had been a nurse with a natural drive and desire to help other people. She reiterated how their senseless and brutal deaths have had a lasting impact on hundreds of other people and how more than 500 people had attended their funerals. Somewhere within this speech, Kim Snibson reportedly began to cry.

Another of McKay's sisters, Jan Keily, spoke of her utter confusion at how Snibson, Flintjar, and Lea-Caton could have brought themselves to do what they had done. She also addressed how insulting it was to the memories or their loved ones that Snibson still maintained that there had been an affair, not to mention the accusations she had made about McKay's intended violence towards Snibson. "The families are shocked by the lies that have been told about Kathryn McKay and Gregory Hosa by the three offenders."

Justice Buddin commended the sisters for the dignity and grace they had shown while delivering their statements before adjourning the proceedings. When he delivered the final verdict, Justice Buddin gave his own opinion on the case before him. He expressed how the crimes against this kind-hearted couple had been committed with a "considerable degree of callousness".

Justice Buddin explored the suffering that was inflicted upon Mr Hosa and Ms McKay, not just at the agonizingly slow and painful death, but at the mental torture that must have endured at the hands of the captors. He expressed how they were forced to wait for a "not inconsiderable amount of time", stuck in a state of anguish, wondering what their kidnappers would decide to do to them. "They were totally defenseless and at the mercy of the offenders," he said.

Justice Buddin then turned his attention to the version of events that Snibson had put forth, the version of events that left her as a victim of circumstances and Lea-Coton's vicious nature. He described this story as "implausible", "quite fanciful" and "tailored to suit inescapable, objective facts". As proof of the ridiculousness of her claims, he pointed to her recruitment of accomplices. This was not an act of a woman caught off guard by a lover's spat but instead was indicative of the level of calculation and manipulation she was capable of wilfully wielding.

While Snibson had told the court that she was sorry for the role she had played in the couple's grizzly end, Justice Buddin was not swayed. He explained that he had not believed her words to be those of someone truly remorseful and repentant, but instead said that whatever contrition she had expressed struck him as contrived. His final verdict had been a jail sentence of no less than 32 years. This means that Snibson would be 60-years-old before she becomes eligible to apply for parole.

The town of Nowra is still healing from the horrors of that singular night. As Paul Leask has stated, "that one of their own was the killer was something that psychologically traumatized that community." The senseless cruelty Snibson brought down upon a devoted, generous couple has only been magnified by the ridiculousness of her plan. For all the action she was willing to take there was no way her plan would allow her to gain ownership of Champagne Shire, rendering her depraved actions useless and her goal unattainable.

But perhaps what is hardest for the residents of Nowra, and all that hear of the tragic deaths of McKay and Hosa, to come to terms with, is the wealth of opportunities presented for people to intervene. Be it out of embarrassment or social delicacy, those who had concerns over Sibson's actions had refused to disclose what they had known. At the time it might have been dismissed as a personal eccentricity, a misunderstanding, or a benign threat, but now blaze as warning signs for the brutality that was to come. Perhaps if those who had felt the inkling of concern had stepped forward a different course could have been plotted and McKay and Hosa could have been spared. But then it is also possible that nothing could have deterred Snibson, and that these murders were the only end her insatiable greed would have allowed. Wherever the truth may lie, it is too late to act for McKay and Hosa. Their lives have already been sacrificed on the altar of Snibson's pride. The only solace that is to be garnished now is that Snibson has been removed from the general population and will hopefully be unable to claim any further victims. But what little comfort this offers will forever be overshadowed by the influence Snibon's name will forever provoke. Those who learn about the merciless crimes this woman visited upon the people who would have been her friends will undoubtedly no longer be able to look at their neighbors without there being the lingering question of 'what if?'

DOROTHEA PUENTE

ERICA BYRAM

Dorothea Puente became infamous in the 1980s for being the "Death House Landlady". She ran a boarding home in Sacramento, California and proceeded to steal the Social Security checks of her elderly and mentally disabled tenants. Those tenants who proved to be too troublesome would be given increased dosages of sleeping pills until they died. She would chop up the bodies and bury them in her backyard.

EARLY LIFE

Dorothea Puente was born Dorothea Gray on January 9th, 1929 in Redlands, California. Both her mother, Trudy Mae, and her father Jesse James Gray, worked as cotton pickers in Central California. Her father would die of tuberculosis in 1937 while her mother would die the following year in a car accident.

Dorothea was delusional so some parts of her childhood have conflicting accounts. She states that she was the product of two alcoholic parents and that her mother was working as a prostitute before she died. She claimed her father was mentally unstable and often threatened to kill himself with a gun pointed to his head in front of the children (Dorothea would sometimes claim to be one of fourteen children.)

What is clear is that she was orphaned at the age of nine. Dorothea would then live in different orphanages, claiming to be sexually abused at one in particular. Eventually, her relatives from Fresno took her in. In her later years, she would discount the fourteen children claim and state that she was one of three children who were all born and raised in Mexico.

Dorothea would marry at the age of sixteen to a returning soldier named Fred McFaul. She would have two daughters a year later. Dorothea would give up both daughters, sending one to relatives in Sacramento and the other for adoption.

Dorothea would suffer a miscarriage in 1948 and McFaul would divorce her that same year. Angry at the failure of her marriage, she lied to everyone about the divorce and said that McFaul died of a heart attack shortly after their marriage ceremony.

She then turned to a life of crime. She would steal and forge checks. Dorothea would be caught in a forgery scam, serving six months of a one-year sentence. She would meet another man and become pregnant again. Dorothea would put the baby up for adoption as she hardly knew the man and could not afford the baby.

In 1952, she would marry a Swedish man named Axel Johansson.

CHOOSING A LIFE OF CRIME

Dorothea Puente would be married a total of four times with two documented divorces. She had another daughter which was put up for adoption at birth. The two would eventually meet, however, in 1986. Her daughter would describe her birth mother in unflattering terms, saying that she had "no real personality."

Dorothea would divorce Johansson in 1966 and marry Roberto Puente, a man that was almost twenty years her junior. The union would last only two years but Dorothea would keep his last name.

"Interesting that Dorothea would keep the last name of Puente," forensic psychologist Paula Orange said. "It became part of her con. She used the Spanish surname to con people into thinking that she was of Spanish descent. It helped her get some clients later on as she would use her surname as some kind of ethnic connection with them as in the case of the Costa Rican Bert Montalvo. She also cultivated a harmless old lady exterior in order to get people to put their guard down. She would tell people that she was seventy when in fact she was only fifty-nine. This con, this illusion would aid in her avoiding detection from social workers, parole agents and even the police."

Married life did not deter Dorothea's penchant for crime. Moving on from check forgery, she would run a brothel before being caught and arrested in 1960. Her sentence was relatively light, serving 90 days before being arrested for vagrancy and serving another three months.

Putting on a veneer that she was rehabilitated, Dorothea began working as a nurse's aide, providing care for physically disabled people and senior citizens in their private residences. This experience put a an idea in Dorothea's head.

She would manage boarding houses and cater to the elderly.

Dorothea finagled her way into becoming a manager for a three-story, 16-bedroom care home in Sacramento. She would marry for a fourth time, to a "raging drunk" named Pedro Montalvo. The union would only last a few months as Dorothea now took to trolling bars looking for older men who were receiving Social Security. She had the ability to put together tall tales, most often that she was a "famous actress" and told these men of her movie roles in films that didn't exist. In these movies, she always played the "evil woman." She also promoted herself as a "holistic doctor" and would listen intently to the maladies of her disabled mark before offering a suggestion on how they could improve their health. These stories would always lead to her convincing her mark to become one of her tenants after which she would steal their government check. She would talk a few into becoming her tenants the she would steal their government checks.

ARRESTS AND MORE ARRESTS

In 1982, Puente would be arrested for drugging and robbing people she would meet in bars. She would serve two and a half years in jail before she returned to her boarding house duties.

"Dorothea struck everyone as a harmless figure," Orange said. "So when she started the boarding house no one in their right mind would see her as a threat. They saw her as a sweet old lady. Her boarding house was spotless, inside and out. You could take a white glove, run your fingers across the furniture and not come up with a speck of dust."

Puente was a meticulous gardener and neighbors would describe her as being "very protective of her lawn."

"If somebody walked on her lawn," a neighbor said. "She'd cuss them in language that would make a sailor blush."

It would be this same year that the murders began. Dorothea had a friend named Ruth Monroe who began living with her but would die shortly after from a pharmaceutical drug overdose.

"She was sad," Puente told police when they came to investigate. "Very sad. Her husband was dying."

The police believed her and the death was ruled as a suicide.

"This is the occasion where Puente learned how to game the system," Orange said. "She learned that if there was no crime scene there was no crime. The police found Ruth Monroe dead and really had no choice but to declare it a suicide as there was no evidence that a murder had taken place. That was probably the farthest thing from the mind of the police. How could this sweet old lady be guilty of drugging up her best friend then smothering her with a pillow. She just didn't fit the profile."

Only a few weeks later, the police would return as a tenant named Malcom McKenzie would claim that Puente was drugging and taking money from him. Puente would be investigated and charged with theft. Sentenced to prison for five years, she began a pen-pal correspondence with a man named Everson Gillmouth, a 77-year-old retiree living in Oregon. Puente was then released after serving only three years of her sentence and found the smitten Gillmouth waiting for her.

They soon began making wedding plans, Gillmouth quickly opening a joint back account as they moved into an apartment in Sacramento together.

In November of 1985, Puente would hire a handyman named Ismael Florez to install some wood paneling in her apartment. She paid the handyman and threw in Gillmouth's 1980 Ford pickup as part of the payment.

"My boyfriend no longer needs it," Puente said. "I'm also wondering if you could build me a box. Say six feet by three feet by two feet. Just need to store some books and stuff."

Florez agreed and Puente would fill the box with her "stuff". She then hired Florez to help ship the nailed-shut box to a nearby storage depot. Puente accompanied Florez on the trip until they reached the Garden Highway in Sutter County. She then told Florez to dump the box into the Sacramento River.

"Its just junk," Dorothea said.

Months later, a fisherman would discover the box sitting on the bank of the river. Police would open the box to reveal a horrendously decomposed body of an elderly man.

Everson Gillmouth.

But it would be three years before police would be able to positively identify Gillmouth. Dorothea would continue to cash his social security checks. She would write his family on his behalf, stating that he was "sick" and could not contact them himself.

NEW BOARDING HOME, SAME RULES

Puente would rent a different boarding home from the Odorico family in what would later be infamously called the "F Street Boarding House."

Dorothea charmed the Odorico family, keeping the house spotless. They thought of her as family and referred to her as "tia" (Spanish for aunt). Despite being unlicensed and on parole, Dorothea was allowed to manage the place and supervise tenants.

But Dorothea's reputation grew in the community. She gave to charities and went out of her way to help certain people when it attended to her needs. She went to a charity ball and California Governor Jerry Brown stepped across the room to kiss her on the cheek.

The Governor then asked her to dance to the delight of onlookers.

In 1986, Puente would strike a deal with social worker Peggy Nickerson in an effort to provide a home for senior citizens on fixed incomes.

"She was the best the system had to offer," Nickerson said as she referred over nineteen elderly people to Puente in two years.

Dorothea would be a "Godsend" to social workers because she had no qualms about accepting troubled tenants, elderly and disabled people who could be abusive and addicted to drugs.

But Dorothea simply wanted their money. By having them as her boarders, she would collect their money first and pay them as she saw fit. Parole agents would come and talk to Dorothea. They would order Dorothea to stay away from her senior citizen clientele to no avail. Dorothea was never cited.

"The parole agents definitely dropped the ball," Orange said. "They are overwhelmed with work but it was almost as if they turned a blind eye. Here was a woman who had a criminal record of forging checks, running a brothel, and stealing Social Security checks from the elderly. Somehow, someway, she was allowed to run a boarding house. It boggles the mind really but shows you how each part of the social system had a piece of the puzzle but no one connected the dots."

Puente played good cop and bad cop to her tenants. There were some who said she was cheap and detailed instances where she withheld both their mail and their money. But there were others who said she could be kind and would praise her cooking.

Despite her philanthropic veneer, Dorothea had an autocratic personality. If one of her tenants showed up late for a meal, they would be denied food. She would send them away then make the other tenants "say Grace" before the meal.

She also did not drive and used a local tax driver to shuttle her around town.

"She had a lot of rules," Dorothea's driver Patty Rohrbach said. "Number one, be punctual. Number two, do what I tell you. And we'll get a long just great. She was generous almost to a fault. She'd tip very nicely and make sure there was enough time on the meter to make it worth my while."

Dorothea had a routine. She would go to the local hardware store to get gardening supplies, then get groceries. On Sundays, she would go to church then go to bars to solicit possible clientele.

"Dorothea would target the down and out," Orange said. "She would go to bars and offer a listening ear to someone who looked disabled or elderly. She knew how to game the system and would give the person tips on how to collect more on their Social Security or disability check. Then she would hand them her business card and invite them to stay with her as a boarder."

"She called them 'throwaway people,'" Rohrbach recalled. "She said 'everyone has abandoned them and I've taken them in.' And I thought it was a charitable situation created for people who had nowhere else to go."

Rohrbach wasn't the only one taken in by Dorothea's facade. Social worker Nickerson brought a man named Bert Montoya to live in Dorothea's boarding home. She had taken special interest in Montoya as the 50-year-old Costa Rican needed a place to stay desperately. He was an alcoholic schizophrenic, a man who constantly "heard voices in his head" but someone who Nickerson perceived as a "sweet, kind man."

"Montoya had been living in a place called 'Detox,'" Orange said. "A shack of a homeless shelter that had little more than vinyl mattresses on concrete."

Dorothea took to Montoya almost immediately, sensing he was a lost soul in a teddy bear's body. Montoya had a kind spirit, he once found over two hundred dollars at a homeless shelter and turned it in. He was troubled but not dangerous.

He was someone Dorothea could take advantage of.

Dorothea would take Montoya around the home and introduce him to the other residents. First there was John McCauley, a loud mouth drunk that did all of Dorothea's bidding. Second was Ben Fink, another alcoholic who despite being Jewish had a swastika tattoo on his arm. Lastly, there was John Sharpe, a compulsive gambler who suffered from short term memory loss.

"Dorothea took Bert Montoya under her wing," Orange said. "Moreso than the other tenants. He liked the fact that he could call her 'momma' and she called him her 'honey bear.' The social worker was surprised at how well he had adjusted to living under Puente's care. But Dorothea used him as a trophy. She used him to show everyone how compassionate and nurturing she could be."

The other tenants began getting jealous of Bert, in particular, John McCauley.

"The other tenants were paying upwards of $300 a month," Orange said. "They would get room and board plus two hot meals. Bert would get all that for free. All because Dorothea had taking a liking to the kind yet simple-minded man."

Dorothea went so far as to set up Bert with a running tab at the local bar. Bert would come in to the tavern, drink no more than three beers, then be on his way.

As much as Dorothea took to Bert as her showpiece, Ben Fink was a thorn in her side.

Fink would drunk himself into a stupor and had an uncanny ability to achieve alcohol levels that would be enough to kill an elephant, let alone a human being.

One night, the compulsive John Sharp was watching a horror movie in his room when he heard a large thump. The sound came from the upstairs bedroom that belonged to Ben Fink. Then he heard large bumps coming down the steps, as if someone were dragging a body. He thought it creepy at the time but didn't investigate.

Ben Fink would then disappear from the boarding house.

No one thought anything of it, however, as boarding house occupants were a transient group of people. Dorothea herself would kick people out after a few weeks and sometimes tenants themselves would leave on their own accord.

Dorothea never liked Ben Fink. Bert Montoya was until one night he did something to get into her doghouse.

Bert had went to the local tavern and this time he had gotten so drunk that he passed out inside the bar. Three of the other tenants had to carry him back to the boarding house.

"The group of men that brought him back described Bert as 'blowing bubbles' through his mouth," Orange said. "So that opens up the possibility that he had something else in his system aside from alcohol. We could easily surmise that Dorothea had begun to drug him up and the alcohol only exacerbated his symptoms. But something had spooked Bert. Something prompted him to drink more than his usual amount. He was trying to medicate himself and forget something he had seen at the boarding house."

Bert then ran away from the home, walking miles in order to return to 'Detox', the homeless shelter downtown.

"I don't want to go back," Bert cried out when the Detox manager allowed him back into the home. "I don't want to go back."

WHAT IS THAT SMELL?

Tenants in the boarding house began complaining about a rancid smell that was coming from the empty bedroom upstairs.

This would later be labeled as the "Death Room".

When the owners of the home, the Odoricos, came to do their monthly inspection they couldn't help but notice the odor themselves.

"It smelled rotten," Ricardo said. "It smelled rotten in there."

"I thought it was the tenants,"said Laura Arebalo, Ricardo's daughter. "because some tenants they would not bath on a daily basis."

Dorothea deflected the complaints as expected. She would blame the neighbors, saying they must be cooking something that's "not right." Then when that sounded lame she would blame a broken sewage line.

But late at night, Dorothea would shampoo the carpet in the room, awaking John Sharp.

When tenants and the owner asked about the room, Dorothea would simply say it was a room that was "cursed."

It was the same room where her friend Ruth Monroe had died only a few years earlier.

Neighbors complained to the city and the Department of Health was called in. They did an inspection of the house and made Dorothea sign a few documents.

But the smell remained.

And Bert Montoya returned.

After over two weeks on the streets and sleeping at "Detox" he arrived back at Dorothea's door steps.

Bert wanted to slip back into the house unnoticed but Dorothea saw him.

"When they cross me," Dorothea said. "They don't cross me a second time."

Then Bert disappeared.

"There was a reason why Bert didn't want to go back to the house to begin with," Orange said. "He openly told the people at the Detox that he didn't want to go back. I think he saw something there. Mostly likely he saw them disposing of a body. Chopping up a corpse. Something had freaked him out and Dorothea knew he would eventually say something."

"Bert had become a problem for Dorothea," Sacramento Police Detective Cabrera said. "He might even bring the police. She couldn't allow Bert to bring attention to her. She apparently felt that there was only one thing to do."

MORE SUSPICIONS

Neighbors began taking note of the strange doings of a man only known as "Chief."

Dorothea thought of Chief as the resident handyman of the boarding home. She had the man do odd jobs around place even though he was an alcoholic. Neighbors saw that Chief carted off dirt and junk away in a wheelbarrow after digging in the basement of the boarding home. He then tore down a garage in the backyard and put in fresh cement.

Then Chief disappeared.

And the owners weren't pleased that Dorothea had put in a concrete patio without any consent on their part.

"One time I went to the house," Ricardo Odorico said. "And I found a concrete patio."

"I used to have lots of roses," Veronica Odorico said. "I liked roses. Then I went and saw that everything was different. I said (to Dorothea) 'What happened? You took out the roses. She said 'I don't like roses.' I used to tell my husband he gave her too much freedom. He said it was to improve the house. I said I liked it better like I had it before."

By May of 1988, neighbors no longer complained of a smell coming from Dorothea's home. Now they were complaining of a stench coming from Puente's backyard. Dorothea dismissed their concerns, telling them that she was using "fish emulsion" to fertilize her soil.

"We couldn't stand it," one neighbor said. "There was a sick smell in the air, and there were lots of flies in the area."

In November, of that same year, social worker Nickerson would arrive at Puente's boarding house to do a welfare check on her tenant, Bert Montoya.

Montoya had been last seen in August and Dorothea would tell the police that the man had "gone home to Mexico."

"Dorothea gave this huge elaborate story," Orange said. "But the social worker knew that Montoya would not have picked up and left without notifying her. Smelling something fishy, she notified the police."

Police initially believed Dorothea's story but returned after Nickerson stated that another one of her clients went missing after being in Puente's care.

"Dorothea was accommodating when the police came to question her," Orange said. "They could not do anything without her permission. They couldn't search the premises or even come inside her house. But she was very polite and allowed one of the detectives to look around the home. He found some medicine vials that looked suspicious. They had names of different tenants on the vials but they were all in one drawer of Dorothea's. Then the asked if they could look around in the garden. To his amazement, Dorothea remained cooperative and said it was okay."

The police began digging up Dorothea's back yard. Initially, the dig did not go well. The police unearthed eggshells, food and other articles of garbage. They discovered some leather-like material, with the detective describing it as "very opaque, leathery."

One of the detectives dug further and came upon what he thought was a tree root. He pulled on the "root" and broke it away.

It turned out to be a human leg bone.

And the leather-like material turned out to be decomposed flesh.

The police then discovered the first of several corpses on November 11th, 1988. They found two more the next day.

"It wasn't uncommon for old Victorian homes to have human remains in the backyard," Orange said. "People have dug holes in their backyards and have found bones that date back to the early 1900s. There were occasions where folks didn't have enough money for a proper burial so they buried bodies in the backyard to save money. Initially, that is what the police took the bones for. A case of an old time burial."

But news quickly spread throughout the town and people lined up around the home to gawk. The crowd swelled so large that the police had to cordon off the street. Hot dog and t-shirt vendors began to show up to sell their wares. One of the t-shirts had an elderly grandmother holding up a shovel. The caption on the shirt read "I dig Sacramento."

Dorothea then inquired with Detective Cabrera that she was going to "go for a cup of coffee" at the hotel. Cabrera himself walked her to the hotel to ensure that no one harassed her on the way.

The detective returned to the site and within twenty minutes, he unearthed another body.

"Where's Dorothea?" his Lieutenant asked.

"Dorothea would pay a cab driver sixty dollars to take her to Stockton," Orange said. "From there, she took a bus to Los Angeles."

The police remained on the premises and continued to dig. Three days later, they would unearth seven bodies. They would identify Ben Fink by his swastika tattoo. Dorothy Miller, an elderly alcoholic would be identified as well as Betty Palmer.

"One of the more gruesome finds was that of Betty Palmer," Orange said. "She had her hands and feet chopped off as well as her head. Police searched far and wide for her different body parts to no avail. They dug and even checked under the crawlspace of the house. It is believed that Palmer was Dorothea's second victim and she was perfecting her technique, removing whatever evidence of identification she could."

THE AFTERMATH

The police continued to search the boarding house but found no other bodies. They still believed that other murders took place and Puente had used other means to dispose of her victims.

"We are getting a large number of calls from people with relatives who have stayed there," the Sacramento Police said in an official statement. "There are a lot more than seven names."

Twenty five tenants of Puente were missing and unaccounted for as the police did forensic work on the seven corpses.

Meanwhile, Dorothea Puente remained on the run.

The search began for Puente and by November 17th, she had been spotted in a Los Angeles bar. She had introduced herself to a patron as "Donna Johansson" and began questioning the man about his disability income. She offered to move in with him and fix him "Thanksgiving dinner" despite only meeting the man.

"She invited the man back to her hotel," Orange said. "He found her charming but declined. She got up and left and he's watching television in the bar. A news report comes on and he sees Dorothea is wanted for murder."

The bar patron called the LAPD and Dorothea was arrested at her hotel. Detective Cabrera and other officials from Sacramento Police arrived in Los Angeles to take her back.

"I'm sorry, Detective," Dorothea said while sipping on a cup of coffee.

"Dorothea, I knew if we dig we're going to find more," Cabrera said. "I know that. I know that."

"Well, I didn't put them there," Dorothea said. "I couldn't drag a body any place."

"I believe that. But I believe there's somebody else involved here."

Cabrera knew that there was a distinct possibility that Dorothea had an accomplice.

"Bert Montoya weighed about two-hundred and fifty pounds," Cabrera said. "How does a person that's five-foot-three, five-foot-four, one hundred and thirty-five pounds carry somebody like that."

Resident John McCauley was arrested and questioned by the police. He was later released for lack of evidence.

The police went on to believe that Dorothea had unknowing accomplices, employing her tenants to dig the holes. She would cut the body into pieces. For the pieces she needed help with, she would roll the body part up in carpet or plastic and have someone carry it out.

THE DEATH ROOM

In December of 1988, forensic police work had positively identified four more victims that were uncovered at the Puente boarding home. The victims were Bert Montoya, Vera Martin, Dorothy Miller and Leona Carpenter.

There was evidence to believe that Carpenter was buried alive.

"She (Leona) was put in the ground shallow," Cabrera said. "It appears that her legs, the victim kicked her legs up. And in doing so compacted the dirt around her legs forming a little bridge."

The mystery remained about the smell of the "Death Room". There were no remains found in the room.

Yet the smell never went away.

"One thing I'll never forget is when I pulled the carpet back," Cabrera continued. "When I pulled it back, the most grotesque odor came out and I knew that it was putrefying body fluids. The thing is there was other people living there. And it (burying the bodies) was based on opportunity. When was the best opportunity to put the people in the ground. So these bodies would have to lie there (in the room) until a period or a time when she could get them into the ground. I was in those graves. There was no odor. There as no smell. But in the 'Death Room', the carpet. The body fluid had a smell that would knock you over....This was nothing more than a house of horrors."

THE MOTIVATION

The sum total of Puente's scheming and killing netted her more than $5,000 per month. In turn, she would take the clothing of her victims and donate them to charities.

"We would get calls from local charities," Cabrera recalled. "And they said they were given bags of clothing from Dorothea. Well, what a great way to get rid of evidence."

Dorothea would be brought to trial and prosecutors would describe her as one of the most "cold, calculating" serial killers in American history. No one ever witnessed her kill anybody but Dorothea would later reveal that she would use drugs to overdose her victims. Forensics would discover traces of a prescription strength sleeping pill in all of the remains.

The social security checks would continue to arrive at the residence despite the tenant being deceased.

Dorothea used part of her ill-gotten gains to get a facelift.

On December of 1993, Dorothea would be convicted on three counts of murder of the nine bodies discovered.

"The tragedy in looking back at this story is that it could have been prevented," Orange said. "No one took the time to investigate Dorothea's background. Different agencies knew different information about her yet no one collaborated. The true victims are, of course, the deceased. They were referred to Dorothea as the 'throwaway people'. People that when she dumped into the ground, no one came looking. The tragedy is that Dorothea was right. But for the circumstances surrounding the disappearance of Bert Montoya, who knows how many more murders she would have committed?"

She was sentenced to life in Chowchilla State Prison and she died in 2011.